STEWARDS of
TRANSFORMATION

STEWARDS of TRANSFORMATION

The Board President / Head of School Partnership in Christian Schools

1ˢᵗ Edition

By

Simon Jeynes

XULON PRESS

Xulon Press
2301 Lucien Way #415
Maitland, FL 32751
407.339.4217
www.xulonpress.com

© 2018 by Simon Jeynes

All rights reserved solely by the author. The author guarantees all contents are original and do not infringe upon the legal rights of any other person or work. No part of this book may be reproduced in any form without the permission of the author. The views expressed in this book are not necessarily those of the publisher.

Unless otherwise indicated, Scripture quotations taken from the Holy Bible, New International Version (NIV). Copyright © 1973, 1978, 1984, 2011 by Biblica, Inc.™. Used by permission. All rights reserved.

Disclaimer: Christian School Management Association is a Christian nonprofit 501(c)(3) organization providing teaching and training to Christian private-independent school leaders and faculty. CSM is not a law firm. No service or information provided by CSM should be construed as legal advice.

Printed in the United States of America.

ISBN-13: 978-1-54564-723-3

Christian School Management

Mission
For Jesus, through mission, with students

Vision
A Christian education for children everywhere

Motto
"On earth as it is in heaven" (Matthew 6)

Key Words
Partnership, Leadership, Transformation

Driving Force
To reverse the decline in Christian Education

Christian School Management

20 Kyle Drive, Ridgetown, Ontario, Canada N0P2C0

Phone / text: (519) 401-2351
Web: www.christianschoolmanagement.org

E-mail: christianschoolmanagement@gmail.com

All rights reserved. No part of this book may be reproduced or transmitted in any form or by any means, electronic or mechanical, including photocopying, scanning, recording, or by any information storage and retrieval system without the permission of Christian School Management Association (CSM), except for brief quotations with attribution.

Dedication

This book is dedicated to Christian Heads of School and Board Presidents who are daily challenged with how to best serve their schools under God's sovereignty.

I am deeply grateful to God for His too-many-to-count blessings.

I follow Jesus poorly but always with the end of bringing his kingdom here "on earth as it is in heaven".

I look forward to hearing the trumpets sound.

I live in the expectation of daily joy.

Thank you particularly to Bill Stevens, who constantly was willing to offer editing and feedback to improve this book. Having said that, he is not responsible for what are entirely my own errors.

Thank you to my CSM colleagues and brothers and sisters on the journey together to reverse the decline in Christian education. Bill Simmer, Tom De Jonge, Bonnie Swan, and Alan Pue in particular have all enriched my thinking through their conversation and witness to the truth.

Thank you to my wife, Carolynn, who put up with me reading enjoyable books on strategic planning, leadership,

Christian discipleship, Biblical exegesis, and developmental psychology when she would rather have been going out for a meal. She is the rock of our family and without her steadfast love, I would not be able to be God's agent in this way.

Thank you to my children – Alexis, Brendan, Jared, and Kristen – whom I have observed throughout their growing up and now moving into adulthood. Their experience of a variety of schools and their reactions to the events of our time have enriched and changed me in a multitude of ways, and almost always for the better. I hope God agrees.

What Other Leaders Have Said!

Many leaders have encouraged me in this process, and some of them were very kind to want to encourage you, too, in the reading and practice of this book. Here's what they have to say:

"I read through it, I thought it was very well done. I would love to buy a copy of the book."
Mike Humerian, Board President.

"I highly recommend *Stewards of Transformation* as an essential training guide for Christian school boards. The book is masterfully structured as a "how-to" guide with biblical integration and exemplars. The Primers provide practical guidance in all critical areas of governance and will foster healthy conversations around effective practices."
Cindy Dodds, Regional Director, ACSI-Northeast

"You've designed it in such a way that the majority of board members will, I believe, find useful and approachable. They are not going to feel overwhelmed or out of their depth. You've eliminated the jargon and have provided a great tool box with easy to understand instructions for both heads of schools and board members."
Alan Pue, President The Barnabas Group

"*Stewards of Transformation* is a refreshing and useful resource in defining what we all know to be true: leadership matters! The book is practical, clear, and motivating."
Greg Deja, Principal and CEO of Catholic Central High School, Grand Rapids

"Simon Jeynes has written another excellent book, *Stewards of Transformation: The Board President / Head of School Partnership in Christian Schools*. He provides a close examination of the most important relationship in a Christian school, that between the Board President and the Head of School. This relationship is vital because it impacts every aspect of the school in one way or another. While a strong relationship bodes well for a school, a poor one often results in long-term harm to a school's mission and effectiveness.

I have referred many Board Presidents and Heads of School to Simon's earlier book, *A Call to Authentic Christian School Trusteeship* because it concentrates the key elements of trusteeship clearly and concisely, which is an excellent prescription for board members to get a strong grasp on their key roles and responsibilities.

Stewards of Transformation provides direction for a healthy Board President-Head of School relationship and brings it into clear focus. The book includes a series of primers, one or two-page summaries in areas where agreement on the principles is essential (e.g. strategic operations, finances, running a meeting, Christian school leadership, etc.). The "Holding the Board accountable" and "When there is a crisis" chapters are worth the cost of the book by themselves. This is an excellent book for those currently serving, desiring to serve, or those who need a better understanding of how Board Presidents and Heads of a Christian School can serve together in harmony, constructive dissonance, and model Christian character in the process."
Cecil Swetland, Regional Director, ACSI-California/Hawaii

Contents

Dedication ix
What Other Leaders Have Said! xi
The Author xvii
Introduction xxi
Transformational Leadership 1
Transforming Cultures 7
The Route to Board President and Implications 12
    Primer: Strategic and Operations Thinking
    (Complementary Leadership) 14
    Primer: Finances, Tuition Setting, and Budgeting 16
    Primer: Philanthropy and the Stewardship of
    Donors 19
    Primer: Facilities and their Long-term Stewardship 21
    Primer: Support and Evaluation of Your Head
    of School 23
    Primer: Running a Board Meeting 25
    Primer: Organizing a Committee System 27
    Primer: Managing Leadership Succession, Voluntary
    and Professional 29

The Route to Head of School and Implications 31
   Primer: Christian Faculty Culture 34
   Primer: School Finances 36
   Primer: Philanthropy 38
   Primer: Christian School Leadership 40
   Primer: Parents 44
   Primer: Children 46
   Primer: Wellness 48
The Board President and Head of School as Employer and Employee 50
The Board President and Head of School as Partners 53
Board Meetings 55
   Agendas 56
   Reporting to the Board 59
   Board Meeting Structure 60
   The Board Calendar 62
Staffing the Board and the Committees: The Leadership Funnel 64
Holding the Board Accountable 68
When There Is a Crisis 74
Board President and Head of School Communication 78
Mentoring and Coaching the Board Member 84
   Coaching 86
   Mentoring 86
   In the Boardroom Coaching 86
   Out of the Boardroom Mentoring and Coaching 88
Devotions to Inspire 91

Contents

Devotion One 93
Devotion Two 96
Conclusion 99
Appendix 1: The Cord Principle: Governance in the Christian School 101
Appendix 2: What Is the Job of the Board President? 107
Appendix 3: The Servant Leader Principle: Christian Management / Leadership 111
Appendix 4: What Is Your Job as Head of School? 117
Appendix 5: The Ox Principle: Christian School Finances 125
Appendix 6: The Mary Principle: Philanthropy in the Christian School 131
Appendix 7: The Child Principle: the Christian School 137
Appendix 8: Books and Articles Cited 143

The Author

Simon is passionate about reversing the decline in Christian education that has happened during the 21st century. It is for that reason he started CSM with some Christian colleagues and gave up his consulting practice with ISM. Simon has been Executive Director of CSM since August 2017. He consults, provides school-hosted workshops, writes Entheos (the CSM weekly letter), and works to extend God's kingdom by training and coaching other Christian school leaders to work with CSM. CSM's mission is For Jesus; Through Mission; With Students.

From 1977 - 2003, he carried out his vocation in Christian schools including:

- Bible study leader
- Teacher of English, History, and Religious Studies
- Being a finalist for Excellence in Teaching Canadian History
- Choir Director of Male Voice and Female Voice choirs
- Outdoor leader in both winter and summer activities
- 10 years as Head of two schools
- Working in residential, day, single-sex, co-ed, K-12 schools

From 2003 - 2017, Simon was a Senior Consultant for Independent School Management (ISM), an international research based consulting company. In that context, he worked in five countries and in over 150 schools, leading conversations around strategic planning, financial planning, scheduling, faculty culture and strategic academic planning, and school performance analysis. He was also a lead writer and author for ISM.

He continues to keynote, speak, and lead workshops at educational conferences that have included PNAIS, ERB, VAIS, AMS, CASE (2010, 2016 Stellar Speaker), ISAS, NJAIS, ACSI, CAIS, AISNE, NCAIS, ASB Un-Plugged, SAES, FCIS, CSI, Laptop Institute, CBOA, LEA, US Play Coalition. He worked with ACSI as part of their LeadershipU Program for two years.

Simon earned his MA from the University of Oxford (School of Modern History), his BEd (Hons.) from the University of Lethbridge, and his MEd (Educational Leadership) from Concordia University. As a believer in life-long learning, he:

- has taken graduate and other courses from Prairie Bible Institute, Athabasca University, and the University of Western Ontario
- attended the Center for Creative Leadership, Greensboro, NC, and is certified to carry out/coach 360° Assessments; participated in the Program on Negotiation at Harvard Law School; trained in De Bono Six Hats/Creative Thinking, Susan Scott's Fierce Conversations, Kiersey's Temperament Sorter; Key Principles of Servant Leadership from the Greenleaf Center for Servant Leadership

The Author

Mr. Jeynes is married with four children, two dogs, a bird, and many bird feeders. He is delighted that two of his children are now at university.

He is proud to be a dual Canadian / American citizen.

Introduction

The Board President and Head of School are Stewards of Transformation. That's a pretty ambitious way of thinking about two people who, too often in our Christian schools, get in each other's way. When it's going well, it really is wonderful. The two respect each other and each other's domains (strategic and operations), they plan well together, conflict rarely happens, and when it does, their spiritual maturity helps them get through it. When it's going badly, it is terrible. The Board President puts the Head down behind her back; the Head can't understand why, in a "loving" community, the BP "hates" her so much; the result is often an exercise of power with the Head being fired or released after a year or two.

Part of the reason I use the word "transformation" is to directly state that we have to move the longevity of Heads from an average of 3-5 years to an average of 8+ years of service at your Christian school. Our schools will not thrive if their leadership does not have time to provide direction and see that direction gain maturity so that it can be sustained. Neither good nor great schools can be established or sustained in the face of constant leadership churn. Constant change due to leadership turnover does not represent Godly wisdom but sinful and tragic waste. The relationship and partnership between the Board President and the Head of School is intrinsic to healthy leadership, and such leadership cannot happen without it.

The leadership of the Board by the Board President must also be to ensure that the right people are recruited to Board service (the right people on the bus, as Jim Collins so aptly said in the book *Good to Great*), and that the Board is moving ahead, following a clear vision and with a practical and believable path of action. The Board's members are corporately both the Head's employers as well as her partners. The requirement of the Board President must be to ensure that those very different functions don't get in each other's way — employer and partner can be an odd pair of functions. As Board President, you will experience success when your Board acts as a servant leader despite having the power to be overbearing as the Head's employer. How the Board President mentors and coaches the long-standing Board member as well as the brand-new Board member is thus a key responsibility.

The objective of this book is to say to Board Presidents and Heads of School that their job is not about them at all — their status, their power, their influence. Their job is to enhance the ability of the school to deliver its mission to each child, and to do that through Godly leadership, wise foresight, practical planning, keen mentoring, and by constantly improving and enhancing their own capacity as well as the capacity of both professional school employees and volunteer school leaders.

But it often doesn't work out that way. Why is it that Heads of School constantly move from school to school?

1. Economics: There is a strange ethos of poverty where it is expected that the school's employees, including the Head, will be paid low salaries with few if any benefits. I actually know a school where

the Head is paid not much above the poverty line for a family of 4, which is about $24,600. I know of many schools where the Head is paid what in most schools a teacher with 5 years of experience would be paid. This ethos of poverty is draining for a Head with incredible responsibility. It doesn't even support the Head's ability to raise a family. It is common for Heads to confess in private that their marriages are under stress due, in part, to economic hardship. There is no scriptural mandate for it, and this ethos is wrong.
2. Pressure from parents: The environment has changed dramatically over the past 40 years. There used to be an assumption that the school knew what it was doing, that the employees of the school were professionals, and that the Head of School was rarely, if ever, to be questioned. Those days are long gone. Parents are well-educated, accustomed to advocating loudly for their children, ambitious for their children, willing to blame the school for any perceived failure, and they lack the innate respect that leads to deference. Whether this is good or bad is not the issue. The fact is that Heads of School operate in an environment that has the potential for daily conflict with parents.
3. Free competition: Where the public system did not used to be the competition, today it is a significant part. Charter schools, magnet programs, online schools, IB programs, the expansion of the AP curricula – all have contributed to public schools providing options to parents that did not exist as little as 10 years ago. Enrollment in Christian schools dropped by 12% (about 900,000 students) between 2003 and 2013 and is forecast to continue to drop. The pressure to compete is real. Heads of Christian

schools not only have to offer superb spiritual formation but also exceptional academic training. They are too often doing that in older facilities, with fewer classroom resources, and with lower salaries than are needed to attract and retain the best teachers.

4. Social context: Churches are in broad decline while the spiritual yearning for relationship with God is unabated, a paradox that speaks to the confusion and cynicism about institutions generally and leaders in particular. It seems that the consumer culture is now in the church – what can you do for me? All of this has made being a Christian school more challenging. Christian pastors and priests are not reliable supporters, unwilling to offend public school congregants and uncertain about the value of the Christian school themselves. Schools are also being forced to change admission criteria and become more outward looking, rather than relying on a closed group serving a distinct Christian community.

5. Understanding and knowledge: Both the Christian Head of School and Board President come to their respective tasks with very little understanding and knowledge of their responsibilities and with little meaningful insight as to how to handle predictable school needs, from developing a faculty culture to raising money to budgeting to enrollment. This is not a slight on them. They have typically been provided little to no education in the process and, unfortunately, much of the advice available to them is either not helpful or will actually lead them astray. Christian school associations they belong to often provide little leadership and little meaningful professional training. They are on their own and rely largely on their peer group for solace, advice, and education.

Introduction

6. Spiritual comradeship: The spiritual dynamic and synergy between the Head of School and Board President (and even other Trustees) is not nurtured, with much of the focus centering on business and finance matters, conflicts, the need to get things done, rather than on cultivating a living, breathing relationship, based on vision, unity, clarity, consistency, and prayer. The idea that this relationship is transformational is too ambitious for many partnerships. Getting through another year is often the defining characteristic.

These 6 pressures result in extreme Head turnover, significant conflict between the Board (President) and the Head of School, and / or struggling schools that hover on the brink of extinction from year to year.

Yet with all that in mind, CSM believes that the Head of School and the Board President are Stewards of Transformation. This can be a regular occurrence in our schools, not happenstance. It can be proactively planned for, not luckily come across. It should be the result of prayer-in-action, not risked through holy words without holy action. This handbook is intended to provide the information you can use today in your partnership in a practical and hands-on way. Our prayer is that of Jesus in John 17: "I have given them the glory that you gave me, that they may be one as we are one – I in them and you in me – so that they may be brought to complete unity. Then the world will know that you sent me and have loved them even as you have loved me." Without the witness of the Head of School / Board President partnership, our neighborhoods, towns, and cities will either not see or not believe the witness that the Christian school is intended to be.

Caveat: CSM serves primarily Christian schools with lower tuition. There will be advice in these pages that might be framed a little differently for schools with higher tuitions. Interpretation is advised.

Transformational Leadership

The move from the 20th century school to the 21st century school is a difficult change. The reality of college acceptance and the assumptions made at the college level, driven by the public-school model of testing and grades, create an environment where both the private and public school feel that there is little structural room to maneuver. Thus, schools are still organized and structured much as they have been since 1894, when the National Education Association agreed to the standardization of secondary education, and 1906, as the Carnegie Foundation instituted the 120-hour Carnegie Unit. This systemic block to moving forward cripples progress from a student's point of view since these old-style structures also influence the way in which students experience learning and teaching. The reality is that school structures are far more resistant to change than, at least potentially, school practices. The following table is intended to illustrate some of these tensions.

Structures	20th Century	21st Century
Student	Recipient	Partner
Governance	Adult-centered	Student-centered
Faith	Assumed and in one form	Spirituality: present in many forms
Job Market	Longevity and loyalty	Shift and innovation
Church Market	Strong and influential	Defensive and fearful
Teaching	Teacher is the authority	Teacher is one of many authorities
Leadership	Command and control	Distributed
Leadership style	Authoritative	Servant
Evaluation	Pass / fail	Mastery learning for all
Space	Passive	Interactive
Buildings	Double-loaded corridor	Learning Commons
Action	Doing	Reflecting
Environment	Stable	Adaptive
Orientation	Past	Future
Attitude	Certainty	Inquiry
Academics	Core curriculum	The Whole Child
Focus	College preparation	College, career, and flourishing

This is not to dispute or impugn the inspirational work done by some educational leaders at the divisional and Head level across North America. It is also not to ignore that visionary work of 20th century educators such as Maria Montessori and A. S. Neill. However, their accomplishments serve to highlight the intransigence of the system as a whole. Even visionary Heads and academic leaders find themselves fighting an often-losing battle against parents and Boards who are concerned that innovation, risk, and vision are good for every school except theirs. "Proven" track records of SAT, AP, ACT, MAP, ERB, IB scores, and the college acceptance list have stymied attempts to change what does not seem to be "broken," even as the realities of the career world and social norms continue to be rapidly in flux. Oddly, excellence is not universally prized in the Christian school industry. And "good enough" is the enemy of change and innovation.

Changing the nature of the Christian school is a necessary effect of the faithful, visionary, and transformational partnership of the Head of School and Board President. The Christian school, as an intrinsic part of its character, desires to be salt and light in its culture and struggles with effecting that in the life of each child. CSM suggests that there are both traps and great potential gains to be had in this salt-and-light work.

Traps are typically negative in their impact on enrollment, financial stability, and mission delivery.

Conversely, gains are typically positive for enrollment, financial stability, and mission delivery.

	Trap	Gain
Politics	Identification with a single viewpoint / party	Identification with the Biblical call to social justice for the unborn, the poor, the immigrant, the widow, and the orphan
Economics	Poverty and sacrifice as the norm	Money understood as Biblical stewardship, whether rich or poor
Culture	Isolation from the general population	Convicted by the Biblical mandate to be in, though not of, this world.
Eternity	Despair about the current times	Called to bring God's kingdom on Earth as it is in heaven
Patriotism	Parallel to and intertwined with faith	Identification first as a citizen of God's kingdom
Change	Looking back to a golden and mythical past	Hope is identified as being personified in Jesus – past, present, and future
Membership	Defined by church requirements	Embracing each family under the school's mission

The Christian school on the trap side aligns and identifies with groups in society, thus placing it in a semi-allegiance that tends to attract those who belong to such groups and repel those who do not. Groups like churches tend to be declining. Groups like political parties tend to be alienating and polarizing. If the Christian school student is to be salt and light, then the primary position of the school must be Christian. By its very nature, recognizing all people as sinners and needing salvation through Jesus' death and resurrection, Christian schools are counter-cultural and, in that sense, must teach their children from a position that asks questions of all human institutions / group identities.

By Jesus' example as Immanuel – God with us – Christian schools are deeply engaged with their families, neighborhoods, and communities (local and global), teaching each child to be involved and hands-on in his or her practical and faithful witness. This engagement is, however, an inclusive engagement that meets the woman at the well, the Samaritan on the road, and the publican up in the tree. The Christian school is both set apart and yet inclusive / engaged – the Word is both Sword and Redeemer, Judge and Immanuel. This prophetic call for the Christian school is key. It is central to its success and central to its witness. Without it, the Christian school becomes merely a shadow of its secular competitor down the street, except that it's surrounded with holy language.

The action of Head of School and Board President in this tension of "apartness" and "servant" is sophisticated Christian leadership at its best. Together, you are faithful to Jesus, serve the school's mission, and ensure that each child is deeply engaged in a society where he or she is to be Christian light and salt. This happens in classrooms that are crucibles of Christian understanding, knowing, thinking, and argument; athletic fields that are respectful arenas of Christian character development, risk, and growth; service learning that is focused on being "with" rather than "to" or "for," artistic endeavors that are risk-taking explorations and insights within a Biblical worldview. In all areas, you are committed to excellence. Your ability to move the school from the 20th to the 21st century and onward, from traps to gains, will be your true legacy.

Transforming Cultures

Whether you are committed to a transformational school as described above or not, today's students demand such an education and are drawn to the schools that provide it. Your leadership has to be aligned with another transformational culture in the school, the Christian faculty culture. Where the faculty have been challenged and have challenged themselves to truly grow as professionals daily, extending their Christian practice in faithful service, excellent pedagogy, subject mastery, developmental expertise, and commitment to each child, the culture is able to move in the direction your leadership indicates. Inspirational teachers have always had this transformational characteristic even though they have typically not seen themselves as such.

Faculty culture is often seen as the most significant impediment to change, but this is simplistic. Too often, faculty culture is relied upon to sustain schools through periods of turmoil, weak leadership, poor direction, and lack of vision – usually occurring because of a breakdown in the Head of School / Board President partnership. In these circumstances, the faculty's work, often characterized by school leaders as resistant, should more often be termed exemplary character in service to the child as it sustains the school through years of failure in the school's own formal leadership. I wish this was a rare circumstance, but experience tells me otherwise. Nonetheless, while faculty culture is the key, faculty cultures can be intransigent, and good leadership helps them become transformative. Intransigence is often a function of fear, and good leadership is able to replace that fear with hope.

To be a great Christian school requires excellence in your leadership but also excellence in faculty. The central issue in faculty culture is the inconsistency demonstrated in student outcomes that represent enormous variation in teachers' skill, motivation, and commitment to their profession. This teacher variation is summarized, somewhat stereotypically, in the following table:

The Toxic Teacher	The Good Teacher	The Inspirational Teacher
Sees teaching as a secure profession	Sees teaching as a demanding profession	Sees teaching as a rewarding profession
Uses "holy" talk to cover up	Lives his or her faith	Lives by faith and challenges by example
Does what has to be done	Tries to do better regularly	Is on a never-ending journey
Sees most students as obstacles	Sees students as the reason for being a teacher	Is a student
Enjoys some students	Tries to help all students	Is a magnet for students

Dislikes being challenged	Engages with challenge	Invites and seeks out challenge
Embraces influential parents	Manages parents	Partners with parents
Sees the job as a paycheck	Sees the job as a vocation	Sees the job as a way of being
Speaks behind one's back	Speaks openly	Listens first
Is not a team player	Is a team player	Is a team leader
Is self-satisfied	Is subject to doubt	Is humble and confident
Should be fired but usually isn't	Should be encouraged but is often ignored	Should be supported but too often leaves for lack of support
Has teaching skills	Works to improve teaching skills and is collaborative	Has great teaching skills, mentors and coaches, and works to improve them

Obviously, these characterizations are more complex in real life. But they are close enough to indicate why faculty cultures routinely fail to push the school in powerful directions from within rather than through the urgings of an excellent leader.

It is important to note that excellence of school leadership in improving faculty culture constitutes largely an extrinsic motivation. Where such leadership is transitory, it fails to maintain its effect. One recent research study in the UK found that only one kind of leader had any kind of long-term effect – the leader who "slowly" worked on the entire system and patiently focused on student outcomes (Hill 2017). This is what the Head of School / Board President partnership ideally represents, a patient working together over time to improve, support, hold accountable, and grow the faculty culture. This kind of leadership develops the earth within which intrinsic motivation can put down roots and mature. Again, I make the point that Head of School longevity is critical to this faculty culture work.

What would happen if the faculty had intrinsic motivation to create the right kind of environment / community where each student prospered? And, furthermore, what would happen if that was aligned with excellent administrative leadership that supported such action on behalf of students, largely undeterred by political / church exigencies and with the long view in mind?

It is clear that the path to such intrinsic motivation is not simple, or everyone would already be doing it. Having said that, it is also true that the route to such motivation is actually known but rarely carried out effectively. "Effectively" in this context means longevity, courage to act, the ability to listen intently, and the will to succeed. Examples of ways in which faculty cultures are undercut are:

- Initiatives begin with great fanfare but are not supported beyond the roll-out.
- New initiatives are undercut by even newer initiatives that take resources and time away from the original initiative.
- Professional development is not sustained as an ongoing and constant activity that is career-long for each faculty member.
- New leaders come into the school who want to make their own mark and consequently pay little attention or only lip service to the actions of their predecessors.
- Faculty are able to wait out the short-lived administrator — their commitment to their schools, for

good or for bad, easily outweighs the influence of an individual administrator who passes through.
- Administrators tell faculty what to do rather than engage in a conversation.
- Administrators fail to dismiss or counsel out faculty who are not getting with the program.

There are many more examples.

In "starved" faculty cultures, the student body is only partially engaged for only part of the time and is convinced that school is an obstacle course set up by adults for students to learn, practice, and play the adult game. There are so many people in schools who feel invisible, and first in line are many students.

In the transformed school, on the other hand, an intrinsically motivated faculty is in a deep conversation with their Head of School (fully supported by the Board President and resourced by the Board) that is founded on shared faithfulness, mutual respect, deep support, active patience, and a laser-like focus on each child. In this school, mission is always a discussion seeking to delve deeper into meaning, purpose, and presence. In this school, leadership is distributed, constantly learned, taught, and mentored. Here, all faculty participate in the learning journey for themselves and with every child. The transformed school is actually a transformed culture where "being" is active, engaged, vital, forward moving, in flow, ambitious, faithful, and hopeful. In this culture, each child enjoys success.

The Route to Board President and Implications

Where do Board Presidents come from? How did you become Board President? The answer is typically straightforward – you are a member of the church the school belongs to; you are a Trustee and a current parent; you are a significant donor, maybe even the donor who is keeping the school alive; you volunteered.

What are your qualifications to be Board President of a Christian school, whether it is a K-8, a K-12, or some other kind of configuration? Hopefully, you have several of the following characteristics:

- faithful follower of Jesus,
- practiced in leadership in at least one other context,
- professional background with an appreciation for excellence,
- servant leader's heart,
- committed to the school,
- donor to the school (it's one of your top 3 philanthropic gifts),
- hard worker,
- committed to growing in understanding about schools and about leadership,

- humble, and
- strong supporter of the Head of School

What do you need to learn about Christian schools? The list includes:

- the difference between strategic thinking (what you / the Board do) and operations thinking (what the Head of School / Administration / faculty) do;
- school finances, tuition setting, and budgeting;
- philanthropy and the stewardship of donors;
- facilities and their long-term stewardship;
- support and evaluation of your Head of School;
- strategies for running an effective meeting;
- organization of a committee system; and
- management of leadership succession, voluntary and professional.

The following one-page primers offer a simple (though hopefully not simplistic) outline of the above topics. You probably don't have time for deep study and, except in areas in which you take a particular interest, that is not necessary. Understanding the following pages will give you clarity in the important areas.

Primer: Strategic and Operations Thinking (Complementary Leadership)

The CSM Cord Principle (see Appendix One) is key to understanding the difference between strategic and operations thinking. The Board of Trustees, Head of School, and faculty / staff work together to serve the school's children. Neither is more important than the other; each serves a particular function. "As it is, there are many parts but one body" (1 Cor. 11:20). Their leadership is *complementary*.

Strategic thinking is a focus on actions that will ensure the school is there for the next generation of children. The Board establishes and embodies the mission; hires the Head of School; plans for the future and provides the resources (money and facilities) needed for that plan to succeed; and holds the Head of School and, through him or her, the school's employees accountable for embodying the mission.

Operations thinking is a focus on the school's mission delivery in the present. The school's Leadership Team, led by the Head, determines the vision, carries out the Board's plan, and supports the faculty (and staff) to success as evidenced in each child's life.

The Board carries out its strategic role by developing a Strategic Plan (SP) and then following it. The rule is that if it's in the plan, you do it; if it's not in the plan, you don't do it. It's the Board's plan so the Board can always change it at any time. However, this discipline around the plan means that any changes must be intentional, thought through, and agreed upon in a formal setting.

The Board's watchword is DISCIPLINE and PATIENCE over TIME under PRAYER.

"If anyone serves, they should do so with the strength God provides, so that in all things God may be praised through Jesus Christ. To him be the glory and the power for ever and ever. Amen" (1 Peter 4:11).

Primer: Finances, Tuition Setting, and Budgeting

The CSM Ox Principle (see Appendix 5) is key to understanding how the Board must think about money. Board members think carefully and gladly about money. In Matthew 25:26, Jesus in a parable describes the person who does not deal well with money as "You wicked, lazy servant!" Boards are rightfully nervous about money. We are not to be "eager about money" (Timothy 6:10). But Jesus uses money constantly to tell parables about the kingdom of heaven. "Suppose one of you wants to build a tower. Won't you first sit down and estimate the cost to see if you have enough money to complete it? For if you lay the foundation and are not able to finish it, everyone who sees it will ridicule you, saying, 'This person began to build and wasn't able to finish'" (Luke 14:28-30). Our schools have been held up to much ridicule because we do not deal with finances realistically and Biblically. The Biblical Board:

- balances its budget,
- compensates its employees honorably and respectfully,
- provides a safe and optimal learning environment,
- minimizes / eliminates debt, and
- maintains a reserve.

Tuition and expenses setting are formulas:

- Tuition = Excellence of Mission Delivery divided by the Number of Students.
- The annual Operations Tuition Increase (OTI) translates into Inflation plus Rate of Productivity Change (3.20% in 2018).
- The Actual Tuition Increase = OTI plus strategic items from the Strategic Plan, e.g., improving

compensation, establishing a reserve, improving classroom resources, creating a professional development budget, adding personnel.

The Strategic Plan is buttressed with Strategic Financial Management (SFM), where budgeting predicts forward 4 years into the future and provides realism to the ambitions of the Board and Head of School. The Board of Trustees approves the Strategic Financial Management projection.

Financial thinking is led by the Financial Trio – Board President, Head of School, Chair of the Finance Committee. The Finance Committee and the school's Business Manager administer the strategic budget and ensure the operating budget aligns with and is determined by that budget. Of course, if your Business Manager has significant expertise, the trio will become a quartet.

The 3 principles under which the Finance Committee operates are:

- commitment to excellence in financial practices,
- commitment to the school's mission and support of its excellent delivery, and
- commitment to stewardship of the school's resources as the gift of a generous God.

The Board acts as "trustee" for the school through the Key Performance Indicators that show whether the school's financial position is stable, improving, or weakening:

- percentage of gross tuition allocated to financial aid (<10%),
- the rate at which the operating expenses must grow to maintain value (OTI),
- the percent ratio of compensation to total operating expenses (70%-80%),

- the ratio of operating expenses to total income, not including fundraising (90%-102%),
- the operating reserve ratio to operating expenses (2.5 months),
- per-student net tuition (is it increasing?), and
- endowment draw if the school has one (10%).

Note: The Board does NOT carry out a line-by-line examination of the budget. That close analysis is an operating function and is carried out by the Head of School, Business Manager, and Finance Committee. The Board carries out its Trustee function not by monthly reviews of the budget (done by the Finance Committee) but through the Finance Committee's reporting of the Key Performance Indicators, actual versus budget.

Primer: Philanthropy and the Stewardship of Donors

Philanthropy is the engagement of people's charity and generosity based on an appreciation of the gifts God has given them and the alignment of their own values with the school's.

Parent philanthropy is the acknowledgement by parents that the impact of mission delivery for their own children inspires them to further invest in the school for the good of the community as a whole.

The outcome of philanthropy is fundraising. Fundraising is always preceded by friendraising.

Friendraising recognizes that people give to people, not to causes. It is people who inspire us to support a cause. Philanthropy begins then with the building of relationships. Our relationship with potential benefactors begin with 3 questions:

1. Who are you?
2. What do you care about?
3. What do you hope for in the future?

In Christian schools, giving happens on 5 dimensions as CSM's Mary Principle (see Appendix Six) outlines:

1. Giving is in gratitude for what has been done.
2. Giving is done by people who are intimately involved with the action.
3. Giving includes involvement, not just the act of giving itself.
4. Giving galvanizes possibilities that otherwise could not be imagined.
5. Giving is recognized and honored.

Philanthropists give again (repeat their gift, often at a higher level) when 4 conditions are met (cf. Burk 2003):

1. Their gift was accountable – they know that it was spent on what they gave it for.
2. Their gift solved a problem – the "new" ask is for a "new" problem.
3. Their gift moved the school forward; it did not just spin the wheels in the same place.
4. Their gift built capacity; the school got better and was better able to do better on a daily basis.

Christian schools that raise the most money:

- articulate a clear case for support – why they want it;
- have healthy budgets – are not asking for a handout;
- have a Strategic Plan – will use the money in a prayerful, planful, thoughtful way;
- can predict their strategic financial position as improving – their plan is sustainable;
- actually ask for it directly within a relationship, not through sales or raffles or events; and
- do what they said they would do with the money and report it through stories about the gifts' impact in the lives of children.

Primer: Facilities and their Long-term Stewardship

Your tenure as Board President is not likely to be as long as the life span of your school's facilities. Your leadership is strategic, in the sense that you think about your decisions benefiting the next generation of students as well as in the sense that your decisions must ensure that your school's facilities must be and remain in the same excellent condition as when they were first built, or even better.

Facilities include both buildings and grounds.

With that in mind, the Board's Strategic Plan must always pay attention to facilities through 3 connected items:

1. Formation of the Building and Grounds Committee that has as its goals:
   - Safety in the present by:
     o conducting a monthly walk around;
     o ensuring that relevant health and safety standards are known and met;
     o reviewing the school's insurance policies with regard to facilities replacement and to business interruption.
   - Creation and updating of a Facilities Audit (see Item No. 2)
   - Planning for the future through a Campus Master Development Plan, including an understanding of the school's strategic property needs

2. Creation and updating of a Facilities Audit that includes:
   - listing of every major infrastructure element, e.g., rooves, windows, HVAC, boilers, heat exchangers, etc.;
   - costing of their replacement value;

- calendaring their replacement on a rolling 30-year basis;
- budgeting their replacement through a Physical Plant Repair Replacement and Special Maintenance budget (PPRRSM);
- providing that budget to the Finance Committee to ensure that PPRRSM is funded on an ongoing basis.

3. Partnership with the Finance Committee so that the annual budget:
    - has a surplus that funds the PPRRSM account;
    - maintains a surplus that is capable of funding the Facilities Audit without debt or fundraising;
    - recognizes PPRRSM, not depreciation, in the budget.

As the Board President, taking care of the school's facilities through this mechanism ensures that leadership transition does not impact whether or not this important task it taken care of. The existence of this Board committee with its rotating membership is the assurance that the investment of the school's supporters in the past will be honored in the future and that the student experience will continue to be excellent every year for this and the next generation.

Primer: Support and Evaluation of Your Head of School

As Board President, your primary partner is the Head of School. This relationship is not simple and has inherent tensions in it.

- You are the employer and don't really understand what the Head does.
- You are the strategic leader while the Head is the operations leader.
- You are the strategic leader and the Head is the visionary leader.
- You are a part-time volunteer while the Head is a full-time professional
- You have been involved for decades while the Head is a newcomer – or the reverse!

Your relationship, therefore, has every possibility of failure. In fact, many Christian schools go through periodic crisis because of these tensions and the failure to resolve them well.

As a Board President, be first a servant leader. CSM's Servant Leader Principle states: Servant leadership has an objective that is clear and non-negotiable. At the heart of the word service is the person of the child. Your relationship with the Head of School is not about like or dislike, it is about effective service to the school's children.

Therefore, first serve / support your Head of School.

- Pray for her daily.
- Go out for a coffee once a week with her and not necessarily to talk business.
- Ask her what she needs to be successful.
- Think of her as a whole person.

- Thank her and respect her service.
- Visit the school for key events and be visible as a supporter.

Then, hold her accountable.

- Use the Strategic Plan to discuss and agree with her what she will be accountable for each year.
- Make those items measurable and agree what the measures will be.
- Identify when she will accomplish those goals.
- Meet with her at least monthly to formally review her progress.
- Ask her at each meeting what she needs to be successful.
- Report to the Board at each Board meeting that she is on target and, annually, that she has met her goals.
- Give her a 2-year rolling contract contingent on performance.

If you can, serve and hold accountable through a Head Stewardship Committee. While you can probably do the above one-on-one, what happens when you transition off the Board and a new Board President comes in? Doing it together in the context of a Board committee will help ensure a continuity of practice, preservation of trust, and the greater likelihood of long-lived success.

Primer: Running a Board Meeting

Board meetings should not run more than 2 hours.

Board meetings are for decision making (committees are for doing the preparatory work).

Format Board meetings using the following guidelines:

- Send out the agenda (the purpose of the meeting) with supporting documentation 48-72 hours before.
- Begin with prayer and reflection – 10 minutes.
- Take 10 minutes for "professional" growth, e.g., What do I do when a parent phones me?
- Set aside 80 minutes to discuss an important aspect of the Strategic Plan that requires a decision, e.g., the budget, the Gift Acceptance Policy, beginning a capital campaign, discussing new Trustees.
- Only after the decision-making part of the meeting, allow a short amount of time for administration items, e.g., Finance Committee reporting that the Strategic Financial Management budget is on course – 20 minutes.
- Celebrate the achievements of the children – 5 minutes.
- Finish with prayer – 5 minutes.
- Always begin and end on time.

Note: Reports are sent out electronically with the agenda. They are not discussed in the meeting. Issues arising from the reports, if any, are in the administration time. If there are 2 decision items, reduce the amount of time for administration items.

Minutes of meetings include the following:

- school mission at the head of the agenda;
- Board mission as a footer;

- date, place, and time of meeting;
- those attending and those absent;
- approval of last minutes;
- approval of the agenda;
- decisions taken (not the discussions leading to the decision); and
- date of next meeting.

Send out the minutes 24-48 hours after the meeting.

Primer: Organizing a Committee System

Committees are the workhorses of effective Boards. The Board itself is a decision-making body that has neither the time nor the expertise to appropriately discuss the issues. Committees are designed to:

- be responsible for one aspect of the Strategic Plan;
- research and investigate;
- scenario brainstorm;
- narrow down and define options;
- recommend a course or courses of action to the Board;
- carry out the Board's mandate; and
- implement Board policy.

The Board President and Head of School are ex-officio voting members of all committees.

Board Committees always include:

1. Finance Committee: chaired by a Board member, at least 6 members with various financial backgrounds, several should be non-Board members
2. Philanthropy Committee: chaired by a Board member, at least 3 members and as many as 9 or 10, should include at least 1 leadership donor, several can be non-Board members
3. Governance Committee or Committee on Trustees: chaired by a Board member, staffed only by Board members, small committee of perhaps 3
4. Head Stewardship Committee: chaired by a Board member, 3 members, includes the Board President, 1 could be a non-Board member

5. Buildings and Grounds Committee: chaired by a Board member, at least 6 members, several should be non-Board members

Other Board committees can be organized as needed to further the Board's Strategic Plan.

The Board's meeting calendar is built around the recommendation for decision from the various committees.

The committees form the leadership funnel for the Board where potential Trustees can be vetted for mission suitability, readiness to work, ability to handle conflict, expertise, etc.

School employees on Board committees are voting members of their committee, e.g., Business Manager on the Finance Committee and Development Director on the Philanthropy Committee.

Primer: Managing Leadership Succession, Voluntary and Professional

Voluntary Leadership

The committee system acts as the Board's leadership funnel. In the committees, potential Board members demonstrate that they are mission-appropriate, hard workers, trustworthy, able to handle conflict, faithful, competent.

The Board President is succeeded by the Board's Vice President. The President should be in office for at least 3 years. As members roll off the Board, they are replaced by non-Board members currently serving on a committee.

The Governance Committee (GC) profiles, proposes, and staffs all committees.

- The committee profile includes the total number of members, expertise desired, wealth quotient (if relevant), number of Board members required.
- The member profile includes connection to the school, spiritual qualities, expertise, volunteer history, connection to other organizations, wealth (if relevant).
- Trustee members are proposed by the GC to the Board of Trustees.
- Committee members are proposed by the GC to the Committee Chair.

Note: "Committees" will include a variety of different people, from parents to grandparents to alumni parents to friends of the school to alumni to school employees. Neither committee nor Board members represent constituencies such as parents or alumni, even while they may be members of that group. The Board and its committees always discuss and consider their recommendations and decisions within the context of the next generation of students, the generation not yet born.

Professional Leadership
The Head of School is the only employee of the Board. Appointment to and replacement of all other school positions is by Head decision.

The Head of School should have a 2-year rolling contract (each year it is renewed for another 2 years). This ensures that there is always appropriate time to recruit the next Head and appropriate time for the Head to find another position once the decision to leave / terminate has been made.

The Head Search Committee is a committee of the Board. It is typically advised by a professional. Anyone on that committee does not have time to serve on another committee while the search in under way. The current Head of School is neither on the Search Committee nor an advisor to it.

The Route to Head of School and Implications

Where do Heads of School come from? How did you become Head of School? Approximately 87% of School Heads began as teachers. The rest come from a variety of positions in the school – Admission Director, Business Manager, Athletic Director. A few come from outside the education industry, e.g., when the Board thinks it needs business expertise. Sometimes the pastor / priest of the sponsoring church is the Head. I have talked to several Heads who were recruited from industry.

Whatever your background, the reality is that there was probably little to no professional development provided to you before you took up your position. You had some kind of experience and you parlayed that into a job application which was accepted. Even if you did find courses to take or gained a master's or doctorate at a Christian university, none of these that I know of actually prepared you for the daily task of running a school, developing a vision for what the school will become, and advising the Board on its strategic actions.

What do you need to learn about Christian school leadership?

- Faculty culture: Even if you come from the teaching side, understanding how to lead a faculty culture is very different from being in that culture, even if you were a faculty leader yourself. If you are from outside the faculty culture, then you will recognize it as different from any other kind of culture you have been a part of.
- School finances: Unless you are an experienced Business Manager, the finances of the school are straightforward and complex at the same time. Leading the finances of a school is both simple (the basics are not difficult) and extremely hard (people and decisions are involved).
- Philanthropy: Asking people for money is just not what most people do! Your connection to philanthropy is most likely on the giving side, and that experience is likely to be very mixed. Some of your giving is probably inspirational and enthusiastic. Some, or much, is probably dutiful and even tinged with guilt.
- Leadership: You are a leader, but there is no obvious definition that you can memorize and have it down pat. Leadership for you includes everything from the mundane (moving chairs) to the highly sophisticated (leading the school's vision).
- Parents: They are going to be your biggest supporters and your biggest antagonists. Understanding and being able to listen to parents such that they can hear you when you speak is maybe the highest of skills.
- Children: You probably, but not necessarily, have an education background. Even if you do, seeing children from the Head's office is a different experience from teaching a class or coaching a team or directing

a choir. Remembering that the school is for each child will be your greatest challenge.
- Wellness: Being overwhelmed is an experience that every Head has. The issue is not whether you will be overwhelmed but whether you are well enough to handle it . . . and committed to habits of living that empower you to live a balanced life and not succumb to being overwhelmed.

Primer: Christian Faculty Culture

Faculty culture is the only true culture in the school. CSM's Cord Principle states that "the faculty serve the children, deliver the mission, and act collaboratively as a professional learning community." Each individual teacher, within that context, "is the intersect (the relationship-in-action) of the school's mission with the child and is fundamentally concerned with empowering the child's agency in interaction with the school's mission."

Powerful research shows that individual members of the faculty directly impact the faculty culture and directly impact student outcomes. An inadequate teacher impacts not only the results of her own class but also the classes of her colleagues (Rivkin 2005, Rockoff 2004, Sanders 1996). A teacher who is unwilling to grow slows and even stops the growth of the teacher who is eager to grow – "spillover" (Corsello 2017). A teacher who is depressed / unhappy impacts both students and colleagues through "emotional contagion" (Johnson 2008).

Christian faculty cultures are:

- imbued with their faith and committed to Biblical Godliness;
- models for Christian living and service;
- fragile – criticism, even mild, overwhelms praise; perceived threat to one is considered threat to all (even when this is understood by the culture as irrational);
- egalitarian – an ethos of equality and collaboration with every member equal to every other member;
- hierarchical – an ethos of power and isolation based on experience, perceived importance, division, and influence (in tension with egalitarian);

- committed to children – willing to expend enormous effort at all times of the day and night on behalf of their students;
- adult-centered – often arguing for what's best for themselves, their team or department (in tension with being committed to children);
- expert – well-educated and with strong interest in learning; and
- traditional – reliant on past practice (in tension with expert).

With that in mind, leading a Christian faculty culture requires:

- clear vision so that they know where you are headed;
- collaboration to include the culture in how to get there;
- a person of high moral and faithful character;
- the ability to connect faith and action so that they are seen as 2 sides of the same coin;
- commitment to the continuous funding of professional learning with a metric of 5% of the operating budget as the goal;
- commitment to a Christian Professional Learning Community;
- commitment to providing time within the paid day for faculty to collaborate with each other;
- ability to model and lead a culture of learning and accountability;
- personal commitment to prayer, Bible study, study of leadership practices; and
- collection of data to inform decision making.

Primer: School Finances

Your school's finances split into income and expenses. Each has 3 buckets.

Income	Tuition and fees (90%-102%) of all the money you need to pay expenses)
	Donations (annual giving to enrich the child's experience; strategic giving to transform the school's future)
	Other income, such as extended care, rentals, food services, transportation (typically not a difference maker)
Expenses	Compensation (non-negotiable unless you let someone go: 70%-80% of total expenses)
	Fixed costs (non-negotiable, e.g., utilities)
	Program support (curricular and cocurricular budgets)

Organizations such as ISM (Independent School Management), NBOA (National Business Officers Association), and Measuring Success) have identified that there is no correlation between tuition level and school enrollment (see the CSM article: There is No Connection between Tuition and Enrollment). Tuition is therefore more flexible than you or your Board think.

On the other hand, expenses have very little flexibility, and both you and your Board are typically anxious to improve the school's quality – which takes more tuition.

Typically underfunded elements of the budget include:

- professional development to support a Christian Professional Learning Community (metric of 5% of operating expenses);

- committed to children – willing to expend enormous effort at all times of the day and night on behalf of their students;
- adult-centered – often arguing for what's best for themselves, their team or department (in tension with being committed to children);
- expert – well-educated and with strong interest in learning; and
- traditional – reliant on past practice (in tension with expert).

With that in mind, leading a Christian faculty culture requires:

- clear vision so that they know where you are headed;
- collaboration to include the culture in how to get there;
- a person of high moral and faithful character;
- the ability to connect faith and action so that they are seen as 2 sides of the same coin;
- commitment to the continuous funding of professional learning with a metric of 5% of the operating budget as the goal;
- commitment to a Christian Professional Learning Community;
- commitment to providing time within the paid day for faculty to collaborate with each other;
- ability to model and lead a culture of learning and accountability;
- personal commitment to prayer, Bible study, study of leadership practices; and
- collection of data to inform decision making.

Primer: School Finances

Your school's finances split into income and expenses. Each has 3 buckets.

Income   Tuition and fees (90%-102%) of all the money you need to pay expenses)
Donations (annual giving to enrich the child's experience; strategic giving to transform the school's future)
Other income, such as extended care, rentals, food services, transportation (typically not a difference maker)

Expenses   Compensation (non-negotiable unless you let someone go: 70%-80% of total expenses)
Fixed costs (non-negotiable, e.g., utilities)
Program support (curricular and cocurricular budgets)

    Organizations such as ISM (Independent School Management), NBOA (National Business Officers Association), and Measuring Success) have identified that there is no correlation between tuition level and school enrollment (see the CSM article: There is No Connection between Tuition and Enrollment). Tuition is therefore more flexible than you or your Board think.

    On the other hand, expenses have very little flexibility, and both you and your Board are typically anxious to improve the school's quality – which takes more tuition.

    Typically underfunded elements of the budget include:

- professional development to support a Christian Professional Learning Community (metric of 5% of operating expenses);

- curriculum development and classroom resource support (except athletics);
- faculty compensation (70%-80% of operating expenses); and
- facility renewal.

Note: Compensation is a dis-satisfier. Giving people more money doesn't make them work harder – it makes them feel treated professionally which is one key to retention and recruitment of excellence. Professional development dollars are a satisfier. They are key to elevating performance and are a motivator for that.

Typical reasons for lacking the money to fund the budget include:

- unwillingness to raise tuition,
- student / teacher ratio,
- under-enrollment (classes are not full and so income is not maximized).

Debt is a bad idea. Debt payments force higher tuition. The ambitions of the school should be met through tuition and philanthropy.

Reserves are a good idea. Every school needs 2-3 months of operating reserves to deal with fiscal ups and downs and to fund replacement of rooves, boilers, etc. (known as PPRRSM).

Primer: Philanthropy

As Head, you have the greatest influence on how much the school raises for annual or strategic giving. People give to people first and to causes second. You are the most passionate advocate of the cause, the prime educator. You are also often the chief solicitor of gifts. You have the ability to ask any of the school's donors for any size of gift – unusual since all other solicitors must ask at their own level of giving.

Penelope Burk writes in *Donor-Centered Leadership*: "How the Chief Executive Officer negotiates the relationship between fundraisers and Board member and in fact, how she incorporates fundraising into the culture of her not-for-profit, determines whether her organization thrives financially or just survives" (p. 8).

To raise money, you have to know your donors. This means you have to be committed to data collection, data management, and data interpretation. Knowing your donors means you are able to:

- address them by name,
- understand their values – what they are passionate about,
- ask them for specific gifts, and
- deepen the relationship and commitment.

Treating the donor well means that you:

- focus first on the relationship,
- if it's a couple, include both persons,
- educate the donor before you make any ask,
- empower the donor to give to values / passion,
- thank appropriately,

- continue to inform and educate about the impact of the gift, and
- only ask once a year.

Recognize that your faculty are the fulcrum on which philanthropy rises and falls. If they are doing a great job, you have a persuasive case. If they are doing a bad job, you have no case at all.

Donors of the largest gifts want to know and see:

1. The school's Strategic Plan (I'm not giving into a void)
2. A budget projection (my gift is going to something sustainable)
3. Involvement (ask my opinion, invite me to see)
4. Accountability (keep me informed about progress, be honest about issues)

Jesus had a group of fundraisers who supported his ministry (Luke 8:3). Philanthropy is thoroughly Biblical.

Ensure that you have clear policies and procedures that govern all philanthropy.

Useful websites include Council for the Advancement and Support of Education (case.org) and Association of Fundraising Professionals (afpnet.org).

Primer: Christian School Leadership

What makes Christian school leadership different from just school leadership? These primers are identifying aspects of leadership that all school leaders would appreciate and attempt to fulfill in their own practice. But what makes it *Christian* leadership? CSM would suggest the following:

- Our schools have eternal significance through our embrace of each child with the love of Jesus, and so our leadership also has eternal significance.
- We believe each person has meaning and purpose — every child has a purpose within the context of creation, incarnation, Parousia, and we lead with purpose in mind for each child.
- We believe that our schools are communities, part of the body of Christ, and so our leadership is applied corporately.
- We are filled with hope — St. Matthew (chapter 12) quotes Isaiah 42: "In his name the nations will put their hope." We are not Pollyannas but eternally hopeful leaders.
- We are motivated by our gratitude to God, who has saved us from our sin, rather than by money, position, or praise, and so our leadership is in gratitude, neither compelled nor bought.
- We lead within an eternal dimension — we live our lives in obedience to the Word and Will of God and fully understand that success is not measured as the world measures. As St. Paul admits in 2 Corinthians 10: "We do not dare to classify or compare ourselves with some who commend themselves. When they measure themselves by themselves and compare themselves with themselves, they are not wise. We, however, will not boast beyond proper limits, but

- will confine our boasting to the sphere of service God himself has assigned to us."
- We lead in the here and now. We are grateful when success is also given to us in a temporal dimension, in the here and now. Jesus himself said, as reported by St. Luke in chapter 6: "Give, and it will be given to you. A good measure, pressed down, shaken together and running over, will be poured into your lap. For with the measure you use, it will be measured to you." Blessings are both spiritual and material.
- We lead in a world that God loves and with people whom God has saved. We lead in love.
- We trust God. We know that He gives us what we need. As Jesus put it in Matthew 6: "for your Father knows what you need before you ask him."

We must acknowledge the tensions in this. Do we not have enough students because God doesn't want us to have them or because we are too stupid to figure out how to attract them? Did our building campaign go off as planned because God was for us or because a wealthy parent wanted influence? Maybe even both? Did we fail because a student failed? What is the boundary between accountability and self-flagellation? What is the difference between humility and an unwillingness to acknowledge God's gifts to us?

This is a primer, not a book on leadership. But I will spend a little more time on this since it is foundational to how "I" must act as Head of School / Principal and how "I" expect others to act who work for me.

Because we live under grace, we are not owed anything by God. He does not have to give us "success" as humans would define it. We are not guaranteed good health, full schools, lots of money. These are not the signs of God's grace in and of themselves. "He causes his sun to rise on the evil and the good" (Matthew 5:54). Sometimes God gives us what St. Paul calls a "thorn in the flesh" (2 Corinthians 12:7) to keep us humble and to ensure our focus is right.

Because we have free will, the lack of health, full schools, and money is not a necessary sign of God's displeasure. We are perfectly capable of messing things up for ourselves without any divine intervention. The lack of students in our schools is much more likely to be a result of poor planning and minimal investment than any divine intervention.

CSM believes that Christian school leadership follows a Godly path without turning God into a magician or a Santa Claus:

- We are blessed with an abundance of abilities by God – each person on the Leadership Team has gifts that God expects to be used (Romans 12:6 and others).
- God has the will to magnify those gifts when they are well used in his service (Matthew 7:11).
- We have the responsibility to act. We do not have responsibility to do the miraculous. As Christians, we should expect the miraculous, but that is not our responsibility (Matthew 14: 13-21). Christian acting is always within the context of a plan that foresees, to the best of our ability, what the intended and unintended consequences of our action might be. God is fully aware of the amazing capacities He has given us, for good and evil (cf. the story of Babel in Genesis 11:6).
- Failure in a worldly sense is always a possibility. There are appropriate fears. We fear God (Luke 1: 50); we fear wasting our time (Galatians 4:11); we fear a community that is not united by the love of God (2 Corinthians 12:20). There are inappropriate fears: when it overwhelms our faith (Luke 8:25); when we are lazy (Matthew 15:25); when we knowingly do

evil including being cowardly and liars (Revelation 21:8). God guarantees success – in His time only. If we obtain it in our time as well, we should be deeply grateful.

Note: Fear is a complex word including many shades of meaning, from reverence to terror. This final bullet is not intended to be exegetical but directional to inspire the reader's own thinking and faith.

Primer: Parents

Parents are not your primary clients. Your students are.

Parents are your secondary client, and they pay the bills. They are also the primary educator of their children – and they are contracting that to you for the most part. They keep the responsibility, but they want you to fulfill it.

The parents' prime concern is their own child or children. You and they can therefore never be "family," however nice that sounds. If you fail their child, they will immediately cease to be your supporter. You *can* be a community where you both have the child as the center of the relationship.

Parents are desperate for your help in being Godly parents and effective in the lives of their children. They won't say it openly because it's hard to admit, but they don't know what to do. Part of our responsibility today is also to educate the parent.

Ensure that your relationship reflects law and grace.

Grace:
- You are there to serve their child.
- You will partner with them and share your expertise.
- You will invite them to participate in the life of the school through volunteering and giving.
- You will go the extra mile over and over again.

Law:
- You will be clear about expectations.
- You will define your policies and regulations.
- You will ask them to be accountable financially.
- You will expect them to be mission appropriate.
- You will show no partiality.

Learn your parents' names from memory.
Appreciate them for their trust in you.

Invest in a positive relationship so you have something to fall back on when inevitable conflict comes.
Pray for them and with them.
Be as transparent and open as possible.

Primer: Children

You are now a Very Important Person. You are not as important as each child in your school.

You have no relationship with anyone at the school except through the lens of serving the child. That's where you meet the parent, the teacher, the staff member, the donor, the Board member. If you add personal relationship to those professional relationships with parent and teacher etc., be aware that your decision making will veer towards pleasing adults.

What you believe about children and about each child will determine the character of your school and the extent of its achievements. Do you believe that:

1. Each child is created in the image of God?
2. Each child is equally loved by God?
3. Each child, while a member of your school community, can and will succeed?
4. Policies and procedures are there to serve the child, not the other way around?
5. The school is there to serve the child, not the adults who serve in it?
6. We must meet the child where the child is?

Collect data so that you know whether the mission-in-action reflects your beliefs. Data can include at least:

- sickness data to predict stress;
- disciplinary data to understand patterns of behavior;
- policy data to see where you are on the grace / law continuum;
- assessment data to ensure every child succeeds and to be able to analyze and improve instruction (90%+

of assessment should be formative, not summative, to reflect grace over law); and
- schedule data to gain insight into whether the schedule supports a child's biology and a teacher's pedagogy.

Report to the parents using:

- narrative report cards reflecting the whole mission of the school,
- student-led teacher conferences, and
- online grade books.

Primer: Wellness

"To my dear friend Gaius, whom I love in the truth. Dear friend, I pray that you may enjoy good health and that all may go well with you, even as your soul is getting along well" (3 John 1).

Wellness is for you, for your employees, and for your children / students. You set the standard. Stress is very high in our schools. Wellness is one way to help yourself (and your children and employees) to not be overwhelmed. Wellness obviously has a spiritual dimension, but here we speak only to the physical.

Commit to the following habits of living for the Christian school leader:

- Nutrition: Determine what your healthy body weight is and stick to it.
- Exercise: Commit to, for example, 150 minutes per week of moderate intensity aerobic activity (between 50% and 70% of your maximum heart rate).
- Sleep: Get 7-8 hours of sleep a night to improve the immune system, cognitive function, metabolism, and life expectancy.
- Rest: Do not work on the 7th day (you choose).

Commit to leading adults from a wellness perspective:

- Model balance-of-life by paying attention to your family, taking a vacation, not returning emails on Sunday or Saturday, and taking care of your professional responsibilities.
- Be intentional by setting up a Wellness Committee of 3 or 4 people who pay attention to school

expectations and advise you when life is getting out of balance.
- Set a school calendar that is doable.
- Reduce meetings by a half and see if it makes a difference.
- Give "permission" to be well.
- Provide a 2-week spring break (lengthen the school year if necessary to make that possible).

Commit to leading children from a wellness perspective:

- Include physical activity in your schedule for all ages.
- Eliminate obviously less nutritious foods and drinks.
- Encourage children to carry a water bottle with them at all times.
- Provide breaks during the day for all ages for "play."
- Do not allow activities outside the school day to happen more than 5 times a week – this includes athletics, music, and drama (for athletics, this includes games and practices).
- Support ending times for activities that enable children to eat supper with their family.
- Support a total 24-hour school commitment (including homework) that enables children to sleep 8-9 hours a night and eat supper with their family.

The Board President and Head of School as Employer and Employee

Technically, the Board President is not the Head of School's employer – the Board of Trustees is. In practice, the Board President is the most likely to have the conversations with the Head that an employer would have. However, the Board President must be aware that she or he acts on behalf of the Board and thus must report back to the Board in a regular fashion. This employer / employee relationship is professionally focused on key steps the school must take already articulated by the Board in its Strategic Plan / Strategic Financial Management. It is in this relationship and the actions flowing from it that school transformation takes place.

There are 2 ways in which this happens:

1. Board meetings
2. Head Stewardship Committee

Board Meetings

- Reports are always in written form unless the Board is being asked to make a decision.

- The Head of School is welcome to provide a written report as to happenings at the school. Unless it relates in some important way to the Board's Strategic Plan / Strategic Financial Management, it is not a verbal report.

Head Stewardship Committee

1. The Board President is a member of this committee and attends all meetings.
2. Probably on a bi-monthly basis, this committee meets to review progress being made by the Head towards fulfilling operationally what the Board has determined strategically through the Strategic Plan / Strategic Financial Management.
3. The committee will report in written form, 2 or 3 times a year, to the Board on progress being made towards the Head's objectives.
4. Annually, the Board President will ask the Board to recommend continuance (or not) based on the committee's evaluation of the Head.

This is probably the most important page of this book because it is here that the term Stewards of Transformation is evidenced. Schools transform over time, not hurriedly but patiently, with disciplined work focused on key items that will make a difference in the life of the school over decades. This patient daily work can seem to have little impact, but every school that has been around for 2 or more decades looks back in wonder at the graciousness of God in providing such riches for the school, bringing leaders to the school both professional and volunteer, and sustaining the school on such a rich journey.

The partnership:

- articulates the key steps in a particular strategic direction and
- collaborates in a formal way to ensure those steps are taken and are successful.

The Board President and Head of School as Partners

The Board President and Head of School don't have to be friends. Indeed, in CSM's experience, it is rare for that to be true. That's probably a good thing, since friends have a harder time working together professionally. But they do need to be partners. Partnership means:

- respecting each other as professionals,
- being willing and able to collaborate,
- being ready to speak honestly,
- being passionate about the common goal – delivering excellence, extending the mission of the school, and
- developing trust.

Actions to take in order to be partners:

1. Have lunch / coffee together once a week (if your relationship is new) or once every 2 weeks. Plan to spend at least half an hour together. This is an opportunity to:
    - talk about the business of the school,
    - get to know each other on a more personal level,

- maintain open lines of communication, and
- build a relationship.
2. Practice transparency
    - Be honest about struggles and disappointments.
    - Give honest answers.
    - Be honest with yourself about your own emotional state and its impact.
    - Confess to each other when you have not fulfilled your commitments.
3. Communicate!
    - Know how to take a compliment when it's all going well and objectives are being met.
    - Know how to give a compliment when you are appreciative.
    - Learn the art of fierce conversations (cf. Susan Scott 2002), and understand Scott's dictum that relationships rise and fall one conversation at a time.
    - Pick up the phone to talk.
    - Never communicate anything important by email – it is only effective to transmit information.
    - Double check that what 'I heard' is what 'you said'.

Board Meetings

Who should be at Board meetings seems to be a controversial topic, largely because many schools use the Carver model, which is not ideal for our schools. As a Steward of Transformation, it's important that you are in harmony about this.

The first and most important policy must be that the Head of School is present at every Board meeting for the whole of the meeting, except during that part of the spring meeting dealing with the Head's evaluation / compensation. CSM feels so strongly about this that it will not work with Boards who exclude their Heads. The Head is a fully participating member of the Board and has a vote. For those who find a paradox here (How can the employee be an equal with the employer?), we admit the seeming paradox.

The reality is that the Board without the Head is blind – the Head's expertise, experience, and wisdom are critical to the Board's conversations and decision making. The Board is volunteer, part-time, and not typically conversant with running schools. Equally important, the relationship between Board President and Head, and Board and Head, must be strongly connected by trust. Meeting without the Head indicates an attitude of mistrust, intended or not.

Second, the school's Business Manager should also always be present at Board meetings. Given the importance of fiscal responsibility in the Board's trusteeship, the Business Manager provides a source of knowledge that no one else typically has. The Business Manager attends by invitation of the Head of School and does not have a vote. The Business Manager has strategic as well as operational responsibilities, sits on the Finance Committee, and is intrinsic to financial discussions and decision making.

Third, for schools that have a professional Development Director, that person should also be present at Board meetings, by invitation of the Head and without a vote. This position also has strategic as well as operational responsibilities, sits on the Philanthropy Committee, and is the person who best knows the relationships within the school. The Development Director's advice in the realm of fundraising, importance in the training of the Board in development, and expertise in developing campaigns (annual and capital) are all key to the Board's success.

Engaging the Head in this way and giving permission for the Head to bring in 2 key employees gives enormous confidence that almost any topic the Board discusses will have the operations people available to provide expert advice.

Agendas

The Board President and Head of School collaborate to create Board agendas and set the calendar. This is not an arbitrary exercise. Great Boards operate with discipline and patience over time, following a clearly laid out Strategic Plan / Strategic Financial Management that is both visionary and concrete. The Board meeting is an accountability and decision-making function ensuring the plan is on track.

1. Accountability: In terms of the operations elements of the SP / SFM, the Board wants to be assured through the Head Stewardship Committee reporting function that the Head is fulfilling the objectives agreed to and that any deficits are being addressed either through allocating more resources or reformulating the objectives. In terms of the strategic elements of the SP / SFM, the Board holds itself accountable to the objectives laid out for itself in its trusteeship of the finances of the school and in the governance actions it takes.
2. Decision making: Interestingly and maybe counter-intuitively, the Board does not spend time hearing reports from the various committees and the Head of School. That is a waste of its time. Rather, it accepts written reports that have been sent out with the agenda and spends its time in serious conversation derived usually from a committee request that will lead to a decision being made. Examples of this are the annual budget, policy approval, agreement to move forward on a capital campaign, evaluation of the Head of School and the Head's compensation. The Governance Committee monitors this process, ensuring that committees report on time and that Board members are carrying out their individual and corporate responsibilities.

Having said all that, it is not complicated. Boards that do this poorly, however, struggle to be transformational in the life of their school. They just manage from year to year. When the Board President and Head of School collaborate to provide direction and clarity for Board meetings, the Board is able to impact the school deeply.

So in April, the Board President and Head of School will meet and lay out the agenda for the coming year (September through August). Here are the steps they take:

Step 1: Read the Strategic Plan / Strategic Financial Management.

Step 2: Depending on which of the 5 years you are in, determine the progress made on the current year's goals and whether any of them will need to be carried over into the coming year.

Step 3: Identify the actual goals for the coming year, and put any from Step 2 together with them into a list.

Step 4: Develop a committee list that will carry out the strategic goals. The obvious 5 committees that always exist in a Christian school are: Finance, Philanthropy, Governance, Buildings and Grounds, and Head Stewardship. Ad hoc committees may be needed in order to accomplish strategic goals not covered by these permanent committees.

Step 5: Write a charge for each committee. Here is an example:

Committee: Finance Committee

Committee Chair: John Samson (Board member)

Committee Members: Deborah Grey (Board member), Peter Locke (at-large member), Chiara Kay (at-large member), Louis Lalonde (at-large member), Kira Jansen (at-large member), Adrian De Vries (Business Manager), ex officio: Board President and Head of School

Mission: To serve prayerfully and strategically through visionary Strategic Financial Management and exemplary stewardship of the day-to-day finances of the school in order to support excellent mission delivery

Charge: To develop a budget; to monitor cash flow; to develop an investment policy for the school's operating reserve

Reporting to the Board

September: Present final current year budget for approval (including final enrollment numbers)

October: Budget to actuals written report

November: Present next year's initial draft budget including tuition recommendations for approval

February: Present next year's final draft budget for approval

March: Budget to actuals written report

April: Present Investment Policy for approval

May: Budget to actuals written report

September: Present final current year budget for approval (including final enrollment numbers)

The charge identifies the people who will be accountable to the Board for carrying out carefully delineated actions that fall into 2 categories. One category is those strategic items requiring Board decision (budget and policy). The Committee Chair will present the committee's recommendations to the Board as a planned agenda item and the Board will vote to accept, amend, reject, or send back to the committee for revision. The other category typically includes operations items that are reported in written form and not discussed at the Board meeting unless there is a significant discrepancy.

Note here that the Board delegates action to committees on the basis of approving the direction and desired outcomes.

Step 6: Develop a Board calendar based on the reporting required in the charges. For example, in the finance charge above, the committee will ask for decisions to be made in September, November, February, and April. Those decisions are now Board agenda items.

Step 7: Bring the committee charges and calendar to the May Board meeting for approval.

The benefit of the Board President and Head of School carrying out this task rather than the whole Board is very simple – it takes about 2 hours or less with 2 people but considerably more with the whole Board; it's not complicated since it follows what the Board has already approved in the Strategic Plan / Strategic Financial Management; and it ensures that strategic and operations partners (President and Head) are completely aligned for the coming year and hold themselves accountable for success.

Board Meeting Structure

The agenda items are placed into a Board meeting structure that should be no longer than 2 hours. If it is longer than that, barring a crisis, it means one or more of the following:

- There is no Strategic Plan / Strategic Financial Management to work from.
- The Board is spending time listening to reports.
- The committees are not doing the hard work leading to the decision.
- A Board member has not bought into the process.

- The Board President and Head of School did not plan the year in advance.
- The Board is undisciplined and impatient.

The following is an example of a good Board meeting structure.

7:00   Call to order and reading of the school's mission (the school and Board's mission should be printed on the agenda)
       Prayer and short meditation
7:10   Any changes to the agenda
7:12   Approval of the previous meeting's minutes
7:15   Board Committee Request for Decision No. 1
7:55   Board Committee Request for Decision No. 2
8:35   Board professional development item (Governance Committee leads the Board in a case study, for example)
8:50   Announcements and any other business
8:55   Adjournment with prayer and thanksgiving

Note: If there is no decision to make, there is no Board meeting.

Your Board meetings may not be currently transformational. With the aligned leadership of the Board President and Head of School, they should become transformational. As Stewards of Transformation, it is your responsibility to set up meetings that are strategic and compelling. They are strategic because they are tied to the Board's plan. They are compelling because they ask Board members to do something important – make decisions. This enhances Board member attendance, involvement, and advocacy for the school.

The Board Calendar

Establishing the Board calendar is now also a simple process. Take all the committee charges, identify all the decisions needing to be made, the months the decisions need to be made, and write that all into a list. It might look like this:

Board Meeting Month	Committee	Decision
September	Finance	Final current year budget
	Head Stewardship	Head's objectives
October	Philanthropy	Gift Acceptance Policy
November	Finance	Draft of next year's budget; approve tuition levels
	Governance	New committee and Board members to approach
December	No meeting	No decisions to make; written reports only
January	Buildings and Grounds	Funding safety items from operations reserves
February	Finance	Final draft of next year's budget

	Philanthropy	50th Celebration plans
March	No meeting	No decisions to make; written reports only
April	No meeting	No decisions to make; written reports only
May	Board President / Head of School	Board agenda for next year
	Head Stewardship	Head of School evaluation
	Executive Committee	Head of School compensation
June	Annual Board Retreat	
September	Finance	Final current year budget
	Head Stewardship	Head's objectives

Staffing the Board and the Committees: The Leadership Funnel

Transformational leadership operates in the present and the future. The Board President and Head, because of their contacts and their experience in the school, have a vast knowledge of its constituents. It is of the utmost importance to be able to recruit competent leadership so that, in the present and the future, the school can experience stability and vigor at the same time.

Stability means that leadership transition at both Board committee and Board of Trustees level is as seamless as possible. Vigor means that leadership at both levels is committed to the Board's Strategic Plan / Strategic Financial Management and thus to vision allied to action.

But finding transformational leaders who will, with discipline and patience, carry out the Board's plan is tough. Many Boards fail at this point – they have 7 years of good leadership and then 7 years of poor leadership during which time the school is unstable and can even collapse. As Christian schools, we seek the mind of God in all of this. This can be seen in shocking form when Jesus rebukes Peter: "Jesus turned and said to Peter, 'Get behind me, Satan! You are a stumbling block to me; you do not have in mind the concerns of God, but merely human concerns'" (Matthew 16:23). Satan is maybe most obvious in his perversion of leadership and his delight in sowing despair and dissension. God is in our own leadership or we fail, and God helps us identify and bring on leaders who will take our school on the next step in its journey.

The story of Joshua, the successor to Moses, might be illustrative in this. How do you replace Moses? If it is difficult to replace an ordinary person on a committee, how much more difficult to replace Moses, who spoke with God face to face, who faced down Pharaoh, who led the Israelites for 40 years in the desert? It is instructive, though, that Moses did not lead the people into the Promised Land – that was to be left to Joshua (and Joshua is the Hebrew form of the Greek word Jesus, who brings us into our Promised Land!). In other words, each leader has a God-given task for his own time. There is a time to lead and a time to lay down the leadership mantle and pass it on. It is God's task to replace Moses, and the method is one we can follow as we take action in our own leadership funnel development.

1. God has already prepared the next generation of leaders. We must also prepare the next generation, following the Lord's will in identifying and inviting them. Moses had the same question: "Moses said to the LORD, 'May the LORD, the God who gives breath to all living things, appoint someone over this community to go out and come in before them, one who will lead them out and bring them in, so the LORD's people will not be like sheep without a shepherd.' So the LORD said to Moses, 'Take Joshua son of Nun, a man in whom is the spirit of leadership, and lay your hand on him. Have him stand before Eleazar the priest and the entire assembly and commission him

in their presence. Give him some of your authority so the whole Israelite community will obey him'" (Numbers 27: 15-20).
2. God's promise is the same to Joshua as it was to Moses: "As I was with Moses, so I will be with you; I will never leave you nor forsake you" (Joshua 1:5). Each generation of leadership can count on God's promise.
3. While Joshua is going to do something incredibly bold and adventurous with the entry into and conquering of Jordan, he is going to operate there with the same principles that God gave to Moses: "Be careful to obey all the law my servant Moses gave you; do not turn from it to the right or to the left, that you may be successful wherever you go" (Joshua 1:7). We always stand on the shoulders of those who went before. New leaders in our school must always take the school forward into a new land and a new way of doing things but always with the awareness of what our feet stand on – the goodness of God, the mission of the school, the Board's planning.
4. In Deuteronomy 34, when Moses dies, God tells him that while he will not pass into the Promised Land, the plan is on track to succeed: "Then the LORD said to him, 'This is the land I promised on oath to Abraham, Isaac and Jacob when I said, 'I will give it to your descendants.' I have let you see it with your eyes, but you will not cross over into it'" (Deuteronomy 34: 4).
5. This is emphasized in Joshua 24 when Joseph's bones are buried in the Promised Land, having been brought all the way from Egypt. Leadership succession cannot happen without an underlying plan that foresees where the school must go. Foresight is an ethical obligation for leaders.

Building the leadership funnel includes commissioning, trusting in God, expecting movement forward while respecting and honoring the past, fulfilling a plan.

Leadership succession is done in conjunction with the Governance Committee.

Holding the Board Accountable

Since the Head of School is the employee of the Board, it is primarily the Board President's responsibility to hold the Board accountable. The fact that they are volunteers does not mean that they are any less accountable than if they were paid staff members. As Board President, you are also a volunteer with, probably, your own career, family, church, and hobbies to balance together with the calling of the school. You can be sympathetic to the needs of individual Board members but not if that means risk to the school. Maybe in the 20th century Board members did not need to do very much. In the 21st century, each Board member must commit to action.

How do you hold the Board accountable? Certainly not by nagging and browbeating! Rather, by ensuring they know what they should be doing, helping them to do it, and counseling those who don't or won't.

1. Remind them constantly that they are there to support the mission of the school.
   • Read the school mission at every meeting.
   • Put the school mission on every agenda.

2. Make it easy for them – don't reinvent the wheel. Have a Strategic Plan and Strategic Financial Management to follow. This does 2 things:
   - It maintains a disciplined and patient focus.
   - It avoids errant Board members leading the Board astray.
3. Make it meaningful for them – don't waste their time. This has 3 aspects:
   - Board meetings must focus on decision making so that attendance is both necessary and motivating.
   - Their committee responsibilities must be clearly laid out so when they are asked to serve, their mandate is clear, important, and limited (i.e., time commitments can be understood).
   - All meetings must start on time and finish on time.
4. Establish a set of Board norms for behavior. The following list might be a good start.
   - We are people of prayer (Philippians 4:6).
   - We are kind and considerate to each other and to our Head of School (2 Timothy 2:24).
   - We are committed to the Board's Strategic Plan and Strategic Financial Management (Galatians 5:13).
   - We are disciplined and patient over time on behalf of the next generation (Hebrews 6:15 and 2 Timothy 1:7).
   - We are gifted (Genesis 1: 27).
   - We are strategic, not operations (1 Corinthians 12:20).
   - We are servant leaders (Matthew 20:26).
5. Educate the Board continuously. Accountability assumes that you are aware and really know what your responsibilities are. As a volunteer with little or no experience in schools, that is a

big assumption. Educate at every Board meeting, educate through the processes you use, educate in the induction process, educate in the annual retreat, always think how any moment might be a teaching moment.
6. Thank the Board for its work.
   - Have food and drink at all meetings (remember that they, like you, are sometimes coming from work to attend).
   - Be prepared.
   - Model servant leadership.
   - Write hand-written thank you cards at Easter (we are resurrection people!).
   - Have a reception once a year where the only order of business is to say thank you and appreciate what they do.
7. Have no hesitation in calling to account for failure to attend meetings regularly, failure to carry out tasks assigned and agreed to, unwillingness to follow Board norms, inappropriate interference with the Head's responsibilities, a spirit of dissension, not being mission-appropriate. Why did they agree to be a Board member (and / or a committee member) if they wanted to behave in this way? Do not wait for the behavior to repeat itself many times. Speak to the issue when it arises. Most of the time, the Board member will be grateful you cared enough to speak and *will* change – self-awareness is a gift too! Some of the time, a Trustee will admit this is not the best use of his talents or time and leave. Very occasionally, you will have to "fire" someone. Know your bylaws and do it gently, lawfully, and discretely.

Note: While the Bible does not speak to Board governance (!), there are not a few occasions when it speaks to situations where people believe they are not "seen" in their actions and so continue on. In Isaiah 47:10, God's spokesman writes: "You have trusted in your wickedness and have said, 'No one sees me.' Your wisdom and knowledge mislead you when you say to yourself, 'I am, and there is none besides me.'" This is part of a strophe from verses 8-11 that identifies the various ways Babylon has been an offense. In a much smaller way on the Board, bad behavior that is not called to account is "not seen" and causes great anguish. I write this note because Christian Boards are not immune to these problems. Indeed, Christian Boards have caused great anguish to their Heads of School, to their school communities, even to the point of destroying the school altogether. Isaiah calls this the evil that will come upon you. This is not a small matter. As Board President, this aspect of your calling is to ensure that such people do not remain.

CSM wishes it was unknown in our communities, but the devil strikes amongst the faithful with glee. We must not let him gain a foothold. St. Paul writes in Ephesians 4: 25-27, "Therefore each of you must put off falsehood and speak truthfully to your neighbor, for we are all members of one body. In your anger do not sin: Do not let the sun go down while you are still angry, and do not give the devil a foothold." We pray that you will not have to hold people accountable in this way; equally, if it happens that you must, we pray that you will not hesitate but, in love, "speak truthfully to your neighbor."

While the Head of School is the employee of the Board, there are also ways in which the Head aids in holding the Board accountable. Remember that accountability is a 2-way street. For Board members to do their job, you have to do your job. We are sometimes mad at Board members because they didn't do – what they didn't know they had to do or know how to do! For example, they typically know they are to be strategic; they typically don't know what that means unless you have told them clearly. The following list is not exhaustive but indicative of how you might approach your accountability relationship:

1. Provide information in consistently formatted reports that don't require a PhD to read. Use bulleted and numbered points a lot. Avoid long paragraphs. Use straightforward language, i.e., not education speak.
2. Follow the Board norms yourself.
3. In conversation, refer to the school's mission and the Board's planning documents regularly.
4. When they have agreed to take on responsibilities, follow up with them.
5. Talk individually with each Board member on a regular basis.
6. Invite Board members personally to key school events. Thank them for coming if they are able.
7. Support the Board President.
8. Collaborate with the Board President in hosting the annual reception.

We often think of transformation as being the province of genius change-makers. As often, though, it is the result of quiet work carried out over months and years by committed and assiduous leaders about whom we never hear. So it is with Board Presidents and Heads of School. We admire Billy Graham and he was, under grace, truly transformational. In the life of a school and in the lives of its children, you can equally be transformational. This kind of quiet and persistent work is both magical and sustainable. As in every chapter of this book, we are focusing on practices and processes that can be maintained from Board to Board and Head to Head. Accountability is another of those so-important practices and processes that ensure the school will continue to bring the light of Christ into the lives of children from generation to generation: "to him be glory in the church and in Christ Jesus throughout all generations, for ever and ever! Amen" (Ephesians 3:21).

When There Is a Crisis

This is not intended to be a treatise on crisis management (there are excellent resources on this topic on the web) but rather some thoughts as to how transformational leaders – the Board President and Head of School – might think about this topic. We always hope that there won't be a crisis on our watch! It could be a devastating fire, an accusation of sexual misconduct against an employee, a hate crime on the school's property, a Facebook or Twitter campaign by unhappy parents. A crisis can take many forms, and CSM is aware of all the above examples and more.

In the 21st century, it is also true that no event will stay hidden, often not even for a minute. When students are sending video of intruders in a school, or passengers in a plane are phoning their loved ones prior to a crash, or an angry parent is sounding off on the internet, it is clear that the first rule of a crisis is that it is not private. As the school leaders, you must assume that it will become public. Since crisis has the capacity to nurture mistrust, create warring camps, bring down morale inside and outside the school, with outcomes seen in enrollment decline or the disaffection of donors, and since some form of crisis will hit every school eventually, it is a significant issue.

In fact, most crises are <u>not</u> crises at all. Rather, they are 'typical' events that we should have anticipated and planned for, so that they do not have the capacity to cripple us. The following examples are taken from real life.

Crisis: The roof needs replacing, and there is no money to do so. Where are we going to find the $200,000?

Transformational Leadership: When the roof was installed, we knew it would need replacing in 25 years. In Strategic Financial Management, we will identify this and other similar needs in order to set aside funds that will strategically care for these kinds of enormous expenditures. This is a Board responsibility, led by the Board President and supported by the Head.

Crisis: Families are leaving the school because they don't like the 3rd-grade teacher.

Transformational Leadership: We have known of the difficulties with the 3rd-grade teacher for 5 years. Despite our best efforts, nothing has changed. Her contract will not be renewed even though she is the wife of the pastor. In the future, we will clearly set teacher expectations that, if not met, will result in swift change so that children get the best teaching we can provide. This is an operations responsibility, led by the Head and supported by the Board President.

Crisis: One of the teachers / staff / administrators has been caught in a compromising moral circumstance the news of which has now spread like wildfire throughout the community.

Transformational Leadership: There is clear school policy, approved by the Board, as to the approach that will be taken in these difficult circumstances. Clear and rapid communication with the school community will assure constituents that those policies are being carried out and that the issue will be dealt with. In a human resource situation, actual details cannot be released, but the united action of Board and school leadership (and advised by the school's lawyer) will demonstrate confidence and sure-footedness in this matter.

Crisis: An 11th-grade student is pregnant with the father being another student at the school.

Transformational Leadership: There is a strong family curriculum at the school carried out in a variety of ways – chapel, family education classes, advisory. There is school policy about behavior that is considered "immoral," and clear guidelines have been set as to how to advise and support students in these situations. This is an operations responsibility, supported by the Board President.

Crisis: A couple of students were drinking and taking drugs over the weekend, and this was reported to the school.

Transformational Leadership: Some actions are provided for with direct responses as laid out in the School Handbook. With no hesitation, the students have been suspended / expelled. This is an operations responsibility, supported by the Board President.

Crisis: The church told the school in April that the rent will be doubled starting in the fall.

Transformational Leadership: The church leadership and the Board leadership meet regularly for prayer and sharing. A community of trust has been created, resulting in joint planning sessions so that each organization is transparent with the other. They build each other up. Issues such as rent, facilities use, and personnel sharing are all discussed with a strategic time-line in mind, resulting in no surprises. This is a Board responsibility, led by the Board President and supported by the Head.

Crisis: There has been a fire at the school, and the classrooms are no longer useable.

Transformational Leadership: Years ago, we recognized that this might happen one day through no one's fault. We already have a location that we can move to while renovations are being made. Our insurance includes business continuation coverage, so the move won't cost us very much at all. It also includes replacement cost insurance so that the full cost of the renovation is covered by our insurance company. This is an operations responsibility, led by the School Head and supported by the Board President.

This is not designed to be a comprehensive set of examples. It is supposed to help you think through how transformational leadership avoids crisis, responds to crisis, learns from crisis, and emerges better than before from crisis.
The first rule of a crisis is that it is not private.
The second rule of a crisis is that it should have been anticipated.

Board President and Head of School Communication

Communication has been touched upon repeatedly in the various chapters of this book. Here, we examine it in some depth since it is in communication that relationship breakdown typically first begins, and it is in communication that relationships can be recovered. Surface communication is easy to do – don't talk about anything important and keep smiling. Real communication risks. It requires a degree of transparency that is difficult for 2 people in a close relationship – the Board President and Head of School are not necessarily "friends" and nevertheless require a similar transparency or openness.

The power of the "word" is profoundly Biblical, and good communication is reflective both of the nature of God and of our ability to be Godly. It is most telling that in Genesis, God SPOKE creation into existence. In fact, the phrase "God said" comes up over 500 times in the Bible. After the heavens and the Earth were created, "God said . . . and it was so." (Genesis 1: 6-7) Creation and incarnation are linked by the Word: "The Word became flesh and made his dwelling among us. We have seen his glory, the glory of the one and only Son, who came from the Father, full of grace and truth" (John 1:14).

With that in mind, you as Board President and Head of School are the communication role models for the entire school community. That does not mean you have to be expert in every area of communication. It does mean that you should demonstrate in your communication with each other the kind of intent and meaning that everyone else in the school community can follow. Here are some thoughts drawn from the communication literature.

1. A conversation is primarily to learn. A conversation is between 2 people, and when it is used to direct, instruct, browbeat, convince, it has become something else. It is often used to prove something, to make a point, to get someone to do something. Those conversations tend to lead to lots of noise on one side of the conversation and lots of silence on the other. If its purpose, however, is to learn, then each partner is equal and each offers to the other. James says (1:19) "Everyone should be quick to listen, slow to speak and slow to become angry." It's interesting that the opposite – slow to listen and quick to speak – seems to result in anger that "does not produce the righteousness that God desires" (James 1:20).
2. A learning conversation is one full of love. St. Paul says to us: "If I speak in the tongues of men or of angels, but do not have love, I am only a resounding gong or a clanging cymbal" (1 Corinthians 13:1). If we think about the content of love, it makes sense – patient, kind, not envious, not boastful, not proud, not dishonoring of others, not self-seeking, not easily angered, keeps no record of wrongs, does not delight in evil, rejoices with the truth, always protects, always trusts, always hopes, always

perseveres. Imagine if all conversations followed that as a rule!

Notice that the focus of these verses is on "me." As *I* speak, these things must be true for me in my conversation. *I* must believe they are true about me and worry less about the other person. *I* am patient, *I* am kind, *I* keep no record of wrongs and so on. This is central to healthy conversation. When, in my own mind, I am constantly thinking about me and about my feelings, how I might be hurt, how I am envious, how I feel anger rise within me, I am unable to manage my side of the conversation because all these feelings overwhelm my ability and desire to learn, to listen, to love.

In *Difficult Conversations* (1999), the authors talk about the Feelings Conversation in this way: "The question is not whether strong feelings will arise, but how to handle them when they do . . . difficult conversations do not just involve feelings, they are at their very core about feelings ... the 2 hardest and most important communication tasks in difficult conversations are expressing feelings and listening . . . you need to sort out just what your feelings are, you need to negotiate with your feelings, you need to share your actual feelings" (pp. 12, 14, 89, 90-91). A loving conversation means I am able to take care of my feelings and my responses in ways that support and encourage the other person and provide the assurance that I am curious and interested in learning from him or her.

3. A learning, loving conversation strives for clarity and understanding. St. Paul says: "If then I do not grasp

the meaning of what someone is saying, I am a foreigner to the speaker, and the speaker is a foreigner to me" (1 Corinthians 14:11).
4. In a learning, loving, meaningful conversation, I am able to manage my internal voice. *Difficult Conversations* says that the internal voice – what you're thinking but not saying – is a "block to good listening" and managing that voice "is the crucial first step in listening authentically" (p. 168). This internal voice is the ongoing commentary on what is happening around you. Even as you are reading this, your internal voice is carrying out a conversation with you – is this interesting, I've heard this before, how will this be useful, did I pick up the laundry detergent, wonder who won the basketball game last night? While St. Paul isn't talking about this directly, his commentary on the internal / external battle for control is helpful: "For I know that good itself does not dwell in me, that is, in my sinful nature. For I have the desire to do what is good, but I cannot carry it out" (Romans 7:18). Applied to the internal voice, it might be interpreted as: I want to listen to you and support you, but this other voice keeps getting in the way with all kinds of feelings and responses and even bad thoughts.
5. A successful learning, loving, meaningful, and internally well-managed conversation is undergirded with prayer and the presence of the Spirit. Sometimes, we give lip-service to prayer and the Spirit, using both as holy language to cover up bad behavior and justify our own actions. But when we begin our conversations with prayer and ask for the Holy Spirit's presence in our conversations, we surely can move forward with joy (Luke 10:21) and with the hope that even though our conversation skills might

not be the greatest, we will be given the right words to say (Luke 12:12). This does not take the responsibility away from us to continually practice and get better. We are both responsible humanly to improve our gifts and spiritually to rely upon the God who gives us all good things (1 Corinthians 6:19). It is in this way that we can overcome the imperfections of our humanity. "Let your conversation be always full of grace, seasoned with salt, so that you may know how to answer everyone" (Colossians 4:6).

6. Finally, include forgiveness as part of your conversation. The first 5 points apply to every conversation you have. This point applies to those moments in your relationship where you need to turn / repent and move in a different direction. Whichever of you is at fault, without identifying the "plank in your eye" (Matthew 7:3) and being truly sorry, your relationship and so your conversation will be fatally wounded. "Anyone you forgive, I also forgive. And what I have forgiven – if there was anything to forgive – I have forgiven in the sight of Christ for your sake, in order that Satan might not outwit us. For we are not unaware of his schemes" (2 Corinthians 2:10-12).

Susan Scott, in Fierce Conversations (Scott 2002), says that this "conversation is the relationship" (p. 6). This time you meet together – each week or every other week, at a coffee shop or in either of your offices – is the relationship. Outside of this conversation, the relationship does not exist in any real sense. If the conversation stops, the opportunities for transformation become smaller and smaller. If the conversation grows, the opportunities for transformation grow and inspire. Having real conversations where you intend to learn through being "quick to listen," you express your love for each other with an unselfish attitude, you use words for understanding and not to spread confusion, you understand your own emotions and manage them well, you talk and pray in the Holy Spirit, and where you forgive each other as inevitable mistakes are made and wrong turns are taken, is a transformational conversation. You are called to these conversations. You lead God's school together through these conversations. You inspire Board meetings and school leadership meetings by modeling, teaching, and leading with these conversations.

As Stewards of Transformation, aspire to St. Paul's intention: "Now this is our boast: Our conscience testifies that we have conducted ourselves in the world, and especially in our relations with you, with integrity and godly sincerity. We have done so, relying not on worldly wisdom but on God's grace" (2 Corinthians 1:12).

Mentoring and Coaching the Board Member

Board members come in all shapes and sizes. Some are executives in large corporations who have enormous experience of meetings, supervision, responsibilities, accountability, planning. Some are small-business owners who understand risk management, the elasticity of the work day, the entrepreneurial mind-set, the tight budget. Others are stay-at-home parents (usually mothers but not always) who "volunteer" on the Board because they love the school – they bring a love of children, appreciation for scheduling, flexibility when the plan doesn't go the way we all thought it should. They know the importance of communication so the left and right hand know what is going on. Some are grandparents who are now on their second generation of children. We have met grandparents who themselves went to the school and are now in their third generation. They bring perspective and the wisdom of age, caution and commitment, and a memory of times when the leap of faith was needed.

Almost all of them, or even all of them, are parents (or maybe grandparents) of children at the school.

Maybe oddly, it doesn't matter where Board members originate. Our general experience is that they all tend to be nervous around schools – what they would normally do in their own business goes out the window. They really want to support the Head and keep out of his or her way but can't help getting involved. They allow their personal prejudices and love of their own children to cloud their vision for the school. They are well-meaning in the best sense of the word.

They are also volunteers doing this on a very part-time basis. They commit to Board meetings (and over half don't make all of those). They are asked to commit to 1 or 2 committees and work hard to make those successful. They are earnest and serious about what they do – their task of trusteeship is a legal one. They "only" have maybe 60 hours a year to give to it.

The Board President takes the lead in mentoring and coaching the individual Board members. We are not here talking about the induction process led by the Governance Committee or the ongoing education at each Board meeting and the annual retreat. This mentoring and coaching is the casual and intentional connection of the Board President with his or her Board members, both in and outside Board meetings.

Of course, the Head can coach / mentor as well, but the power dynamic of the employer (Board) and employee (Head) can create an uneasy situation. It all depends on the individual relationship between the Head and the Board member. For some it will work; for others, it won't. For the Board President though, it is a responsibility.

Fortunately, the need for coaching and mentoring decreases as the Board member gains experience, although there is no time when it becomes completely unnecessary. However, it does mean that what might seem overwhelming initially (I have to coach / mentor every Board member) becomes manageable (I have to coach / mentor our 3 new Board members with persistence and the others as need be).

We define coaching and mentoring in these ways:

Coaching

This is focused on task and performance – how effectively the Trustee carries out the jobs assigned by the Board or Board Committee. It is connected to teaching where the Board President, in helping the Board member with the task, teaches skills and processes needed for success.

Mentoring

This is focused on long-term leadership development of the individual and increase of school-related wisdom that can be applied year to year in different circumstances. It is connected to counseling where the Board President, in helping the Board member with leadership, reflects back to the Board member in order to improve self-awareness and self-confidence.

In the Boardroom Coaching

Mentoring doesn't typically happen in the boardroom since it is very personal and often confidential. Coaching, on the other hand, is the Board President's attitude to running the Board. You can operate the Board in a purely business way – go through the agenda and leave. But a coaching stance makes the Board meeting a learning situation for everyone, with the intent that by the end of every meeting the Board is now better equipped to carry out its Strategic Plan / Strategic Financial Management. Of course, coaching can be done by anybody and will happen naturally. The Board President supports this through leading by example.

Examples include:
- Information: Stop to "remember" facts and figures as well as past experience. Discussions can be

derailed when emotion and personal preference obscure the information that has been shared in the current or previous meetings. Coaching trains the Board members to keep such information in front of them (binder / electronically) and to refer to it in their suggestions and opinions.

Note: Experience is never invoked to stop progress; it may invite caution and avoidance of the same mistakes; it must never be a conversation-stopper (e.g., "We tried this before and it didn't work.").

- Process: Stop to "remind" the Board member of the norms agreed to by the Board. For example, "We agreed to let everyone around the table speak first about decision topics before opening it up to debate – 2 members have not yet spoken." In one sense, this is just you as Board President invoking order. As a coach, however, this is not approached legalistically but as education of the member as to what the norms are so that meetings go more and more effectively.
- Mission reference: Ask the question, "In what way(s) does this further the mission of the school?" This is an excellent coaching question because it places the emphasis of conversation and decision making within the right context. While many conversations and decisions may be justifiable, *only those that are attuned to the school's mission* are "right."
- Strategic Plan / Strategic Financial Management: Referencing the Board's plan on an irritatingly regular basis keeps each member's disciplined focus on what is critical to the school today. From a coaching standpoint, every new Board member has to be inculcated into the strategic culture of the Board, recognizing and buying into the self-imposed limitations of the plan.

- Christian school: Coach Board members in the dual reality that secular processes (e.g., budget) might be the same for all schools, but the Christian Board must begin from a different place. If we are to be a Christian school, what makes the budget Christian or the construction project Christian? Yes, we begin with prayer. Yes, we hope to discern God's will for the school. Yes, we also have different potential outcomes that reflect our Christian calling.

Out of the Boardroom Mentoring and Coaching

Coaching outside the boardroom includes the bullets above as well as sharing knowledge gleaned by the Board President (and other experienced Board members) about committee work, financial skills and processes, and the like. Coaching is usually carried out within the committee setting, and the Board President is only one of maybe many who can do this.

More important for the Board President is mentoring Board members as they grow into their Board roles, including more experienced Board members as they come across situations they have not experienced before or a Board member who is just making poor decisions. Remember that mentoring is long-term leadership development, self-awareness, and self-confidence. It is not carried out from a position of authority. It is carried out because the Board President is uniquely placed to mentor, given the special relationship with the Head of School and thus knowledge of the school, the President's own experience, longevity of leadership practice, and spiritual maturity evidenced in word and deed.

Remember, this is not coaching the task. It is mentoring the person. Mentoring might include:

- Listening with empathy: The key here is getting Board members to speak reflectively about their experience, their joys, and their worries. Listening requires a grasp of open-ended questioning such as:
    - Who is it you really want to be on the Board? (interrogating growth)
    - What do you think you are doing really well that is furthering the mission of the school? (noticing and accepting gifts)
    - What are you not doing well that you would like to improve? (self-knowledge, self-awareness, and self-management)
    - Where do you need the most help, and how can I help you? (relationship)
- Encouraging questions: Teach the Board members to ask you questions such as:
    - What would you do if you were me? (sharing challenges)
    - What used to be your greatest weaknesses? (probing self-awareness)
    - Can you help me to think through what to do differently next time? (reflecting)
    - Could you give me feedback to improve my . . .? (gaining wisdom)
    - Can you tell me of a time when you had to recover from . . .? (the power of story)
- Encouraging learning
    - Provide advice when asked for it.
    - Send materials that you come across on your own learning journey.
    - Invite Board members to seminars / webinars with you.
- Encouraging balance
    - Share how you maintain balance between family, church, career, and Board work.

- Express interest in their methods of achieving balance.
- Pray with the Board member.
• Developing a plan
    - If appropriate, sit with the Board member and develop a leadership plan for the person's involvement with the Board.
    - Recognize that their involvement is a benefit to their career and that the skills learned in volunteer work can have significant crossover impact in other areas of life.

Mentoring and coaching are important aspects of a Board President's task. They are typically integrated into what you would do anyway. Recognizing them as discrete skills and responsibilities will help you make them intentional and effective in an ongoing way. Your impact will be transformational in the lives of individuals.

Devotions to Inspire

Before a really important conversation, it is wise to stop and reflect. As Board President and Head of School, you both face challenging situations that you can't duck but must lead through. You often feel inadequate, particularly when dealing with human resource issues that don't have black or white answers. You can feel insecure if you know that the 2 of you are far apart on the issue at hand. You might be feeling anger because the conversation is about conflict that has nothing to do with you and could easily have been avoided. You might be experiencing the temptation to pass judgment.

We humbly provide 2 devotions to help you prepare for these kinds of conversations. We hope that they will inspire you to write your own. You could send them to us at CSM – christianschoolmanagement@gmail.com – so they can inspire other school leaders! We pray that they will help prepare your hearts and minds for the task ahead (Philippians 4:7).

The sequence for each devotion is:

- a Psalm to be read aloud responsively or together, as you wish;
- a meditation;

- a reading in the voice of Jesus;
- silence for reflection and speaking from the heart; and
- a closing prayer.

Make sure you take time to read slowly and to permit silence. It is in the silence that we hear the whisper of the voice of God (1 Kings 19: 11-14).

Devotion One

Psalm 32
Of David.

"Blessed is the one whose transgressions are forgiven, whose sins are covered.

"Blessed is the one whose sin the LORD does not count against them and in whose spirit is no deceit.

"When I kept silent, my bones wasted away through my groaning all day long.

"For day and night your hand was heavy on me; my strength was sapped as in the heat of summer. (Pause to reflect)

"Then I acknowledged my sin to you and did not cover up my iniquity. I said, "I will confess my transgressions to the LORD." And you forgave the guilt of my sin. (Pause to reflect)

"Therefore let all the faithful pray to you while you may be found; surely the rising of the mighty waters will not reach them.

"You are my hiding place; you will protect me from trouble and surround me with songs of deliverance. (Pause to reflect)

"I will instruct you and teach you in the way you should go; I will counsel you with my loving eye on you.

"Do not be like the horse or the mule, which have no understanding but must be controlled by bit and bridle or they will not come to you.

"Many are the woes of the wicked, but the LORD's unfailing love surrounds the one who trusts in him.

"Rejoice in the LORD and be glad, you righteous; sing, all you who are upright in heart!" (Pause to reflect)

Meditation

Being a perfect leader is beyond me. Nonetheless, I rejoice in God.
I make many mistakes as a leader. Nonetheless, I am loved by God.
Sometimes I feel overwhelmed by the tasks I have to do. Nonetheless, I am taught by God.
There are times when I have to force myself out of bed. Nonetheless, I freely serve God.
My school is opposed to the culture it serves. Nonetheless, I trust God.

The Words of Jesus

"But go and learn what this means: 'I desire mercy, not sacrifice.' For I have not come to call the righteous, but sinners" (Matthew 9:13).

"Let the little children come to me, and do not hinder them, for the kingdom of God belongs to such as these" (Luke 18:16).

"I am the bread of life. Whoever comes to me will never go hungry, and whoever believes in me will never be thirsty. All those the Father gives me will come to me, and whoever comes to me I will never drive away. And this is the will of him who sent me, that I shall lose none of all those he has given me, but raise them up at the last day" (John 6:35, 37, 39).

Silence for Reflection and Speaking from the Heart

Closing Prayer

Almighty and Everlasting God, we are just ordinary people trying to be a great Board President and Head of School. Give us grace to use the gifts you have given us from before our mother's womb in order to be extraordinary. With you, all things are possible. Calm our fears, reduce our anxieties, increase our faith, sharpen our brains, fill us with love. May our meeting together be a blessing to us and to the school we serve. Let us keep its mission and your call on our lives ever before us as we talk and plan. We pray all these things through Jesus Christ our Lord, who lives and reigns with you and the Holy Spirit, one God, for ever and ever. Amen.

Devotion Two

Psalm 63
A psalm of David, when he was in the Desert of Judah

"You, God, are my God, earnestly I seek you; I thirst for you, my whole being longs for you, in a dry and parched land where there is no water. (Pause to reflect)

"I have seen you in the sanctuary and beheld your power and your glory.

"Because your love is better than life, my lips will glorify you.

"I will praise you as long as I live, and in your name I will lift up my hands.

"I will be fully satisfied as with the richest of foods; with singing lips my mouth will praise you.

"On my bed I remember you; I think of you through the watches of the night.

"Because you are my help, I sing in the shadow of your wings.

"I cling to you; your right hand upholds me. (Pause to reflect)

"Those who want to kill me will be destroyed; they will go down to the depths of the earth.

"They will be given over to the sword and become food for jackals.

"But the king will rejoice in God; all who swear by God will glory in him, while the mouths of liars will be silenced."

Meditation

There are times when we feel as if we are in a desert or wilderness. Everything is dreary and there is, we think, nothing to sustain us. Those are times when we need to long for you even more than usual.

There are times when everything is going well for us. Our enrollment is up. Our finances look good. Our parents are happy. The Board is united. Those are times when we should feel fully satisfied and not greedy for more.

There are even times when it feels as if everything is going badly. Rumors are spreading. The neighbors are complaining. There have already been 3 phone calls this morning. Those are times when we need your assurance that the victory is already won.

There are times when I am alone. I might be physically, emotionally, or spiritually alone. I might even feel as if you are not here. Those are times when I must move towards you and trust your word that you love me and that you hold me tight in your hand.

The Words of Jesus

> "*Abba*, Father, everything is possible for you. Take this cup from me. Yet not what I will, but what you will" (Mark 14:16).

> "Come to me, all you who are weary and burdened, and I will give you rest. Take my yoke upon you and learn from me, for I am gentle and humble in heart, and you will find rest for your souls. For my yoke is easy and my burden is light" (Matthew 11: 28-30).

> "Blessed are you who are poor, for yours is the kingdom of God.

"Blessed are you who hunger now, for you will be satisfied.

"Blessed are you who weep now, for you will laugh.

"Blessed are you when people hate you, when they exclude you and insult you and reject your name as evil, because of the Son of Man.

"Rejoice in that day and leap for joy, because great is your reward in heaven" (Luke 6: 20-23).

Silence for Reflection and Speaking from the Heart

Closing Prayer

Almighty and Everlasting God, we lead a school through different phases of life. Give us confidence to lead with your Spirit whether we are in a desert and nothing seems to be working, or whether we are in the king's palace and everything we touch turns to gold. Let us know that as we struggle, you hold us tight in your hand, that as we are confused, we can discern the way forward with your guidance, that as we use the gifts of leadership you have given us, our school will flourish. May we be your hands to do your will. We pray all these things through Jesus Christ our Lord, who lives and reigns with you and the Holy Spirit, one God, for ever and ever. Amen.

Conclusion

CSM makes no claim that we have covered everything in the Board President / Head of School relationship. What we do claim is that the topics covered here, and the way in which each topic is covered, will help you see yourselves as Stewards of Transformation.

In 2 Corinthians 3, St. Paul writes: "You yourselves are our letter, written on our hearts, known and read by everyone. You show that you are a letter from Christ, the result of our ministry, written not with ink but with the Spirit of the living God, not on tablets of stone but on tablets of human hearts. Such confidence we have through Christ before God. Not that we are competent in ourselves to claim anything for ourselves, but our competence comes from God. He has made us competent as ministers of a new covenant – not of the letter but of the Spirit; for the letter kills, but the Spirit gives life." We really do want you to see yourselves as having a ministry written on "tablets of human hearts," firstly in the lives of the children you serve as leaders, and then in the lives of the volunteers who sit on the Board and on committees who have been called by the Spirit to give "life."

Schools have no right to exist. The Christian school equally has no right to exist. It comes to life because of God's inspiration in the lives of human beings who work hard and long to accomplish a vision.

Your task as Stewards of Transformation is to channel the inspiration of God in each new era, to lead the school on a path it has not yet trod, to show courage and wisdom in meeting the needs of this generation of students, and to demonstrate foresight and planning in ensuring the healthy life of the school for generations yet to come.

We can be confident in our calling because we have already been justified and live in the hope of what is and what is to come: "Therefore, since we have been justified through faith, we have peace with God through our Lord Jesus Christ, through whom we have gained access by faith into this grace in which we now stand. And we boast in the hope of the glory of God. Not only so, but we also glory in our sufferings, because we know that suffering produces perseverance; perseverance, character; and character, hope. And hope does not put us to shame, because God's love has been poured out into our hearts through the Holy Spirit, who has been given to us" (Romans 5: 1-5).

Appendix 1: The Cord Principle: Governance in the Christian School

Ecclesiastes 4: 12 (NIV)
"A cord of 3 strands is not quickly broken."

The Christian school includes 3 organizational partners who work in service to the school's students:

1. The Board establishes the mission, hires the Head of School, plans for the future, and provides the resources (money and facilities) needed for that plan to succeed.
2. The Administration, led by the Head, determines the vision, carries out the Board's plan, and supports the faculty to success.
3. The faculty serve the children, deliver the mission, and act collaboratively as a professional learning community. The staff support both Administration and faculty by engaging with resources and planning for their effective deployment.

In the same way, the Christian school includes 3 human partners who cooperate in service to the child:

1. The parent(s) to whom God gives the responsibility of unity (the "two shall be one," reflecting the unity of God) within which the child grows safely, and through which the child, known by God from before the womb, can fully develop God's intent for her or his life.
2. The teacher, who is the intersect (the relationship-in-action) of the school's mission with the child and who is fundamentally concerned with empowering the child's agency in interaction with the school's mission.
3. The Head, who stands as the guardian of the child's healthy development, the proactive partner with the parent, and the sustainer of the teacher's Godly genius.

Together, these 2 sets of 3 strands (organizational and human) are effective, and the school operates harmoniously. In conflict, or where the parts do not lift up each other's sphere, the school is in disarray and mission delivery is endangered. Let us discuss each of these in turn.

The Board of Trustees: This entity (sometimes also called the Board of Directors or Governing Board) has clear responsibilities and clear boundaries. *BoardSource* (Ten Basic Responsibilities of Nonprofit Boards 2015) writes that "strong Board leadership is fundamental to a strong and effective organization" (p.11). This strong leadership is often construed as running the school. Nothing could be further from the truth or more destructive. We encounter far too many Christian schools where the Board continuously interferes with the operations side of the fence, directing school employees and negating the authority of the Head. This has also led the

Appendix 1: The Cord Principle: Governance in the Christian School

Board to arbitrarily dismiss the Head, even in the middle of a contract, and assume the Head's responsibilities at the Board level. The Cord Principle is emphatic that the Board's sphere is strategic: establishing the school's mission and using it "as the first frame of reference when making decisions" (p. 21); hiring the Head, who is the Board's ONLY employee, who must then be supported and evaluated (ch. 3); setting the school's "strategic direction" together with the Head and using that direction "for budgeting and other priorities" (p.39).

There are, of course, other considerations for the Board – but if it can focus and do these 3 things brilliantly, the Board members can sleep easily at night. These tasks constitute the strategic function of the Board and can be contrasted with the operations function, which the Board is incompetent to carry out. This is an important understanding for individual Board members and the Board as a whole – as volunteers from many walks of life, the perspectives each brings to the collective table are invaluable. However, none is actually skilled in running a school and in running THIS school.

To avoid the "blind leading the blind" (Luke 6:39), the Board, for example, approves the budget, but the Head spends it; the Board identifies strategic priorities, but the Head executes them; the Board approves construction, but the construction company builds the building. The Board cord is both a strength and a potential noose – wise Board leadership understands the strategic / operations difference and leads strategically. This makes it a healthy organizational partner and allows it to contribute meaningfully to a strong and healthy school.

The second organizational partner is the Administration. It doesn't matter how small or large your school is and thus how many people are in the Administration. In some very small schools, it might be the Head, an admission / marketing part-time person, and a bookkeeper. In very large schools, the Administration might include the Head, a Chief

Financial Officer, a Division Head or Principal of each division, an Admission Director, a Marketing Director, a Director of Development, an Athletics Director, and a Director of Guidance and College Counseling.

Wherever your school is, the Administration's task is as well defined as the Board's: deliver the mission with excellence, carry out the strategic plan together with its financial framework, be disciplined around the budget, maintain a safe school. And it is clear how this works – the Board determines the budget (and thus sets tuition) while the Administration spends the budget; the Board creates the strategic plan and the budget to support it while the Administration implements; the Board creates and / or affirms the mission while the Administration interprets the mission in the light of everyday realities and uses it to guide and direct conversation and decision making. The Administration must be competent to run the school and, because no one was born with the skills to do such a complex thing, the Administration must also be committed to continuous improvement, thinking about administrative duties along spiritual, financial, organizational, curricular, and human resource lines and seeking to learn every day.

This is excellent modeling for the third organizational partner, the faculty and staff. Their primary task is to deliver the mission directly to the students / children of the school. This is sometimes lost on administrators who, being student-centered (cf. The Child Principle) think that they are also carrying out that task. Well, to some extent they are right. But they are not the Kindergarten teacher rolling on the floor all day with 5-year-olds or the music teacher working with choirs of 60 or 160 children in preparation for a worship service or a Christmas celebration. No, it is the teachers and the front-line staff (the assistants and the janitors and the lunch folks) who interact on a daily and minute-to-minute basis with the school's reason-for-existence, the children. Neither the Board nor the Administration can do those jobs, which are incredibly taxing and not always well compensated. We thus consider this partner the most *important* of the 3. The other 2 partners, Board and Administration, therefore have as their focus the support of the faculty and staff, and all they do is geared to that end.

The responsibility placed on the faculty and staff is glorious and also daunting: "The student is not above the teacher, but everyone who is fully trained will be like their teacher" (Luke 6:40). Their character and expertise must be beyond reproach. The science teacher, for example, must understand and really know science as well as be a Godly person. The 2 aspects of character and expertise must be constantly sought for and, as for all the partners, must be expanded through continuous professional renewal of body, soul, mind, and heart.

The 3 human partners form a cord within and around the 3 organizational partners and, of course, there is overlap. While these principles are primarily focused on the excellent operations of Christian schools, we must always remember that the students come to school, but they belong to their families. At the same time, this is a complicated relationship because the government has mandated that the child be educated, although that can happen in a variety of ways – home schooling, public and private schooling, to identify the basic methods. So the government mandates, the parent chooses, and the student goes to school. What is the importance then of the parent, and how does the parent fit into the cord?

There have been many learned books and articles written about this, and we make no effort to replicate or compete with them. We take a very practical stance. Parents are responsible for their children: "Children, obey your parents in the Lord for this is right" (Ephesians 6:1). And they are distinct from them: "Parents are not to be put to death for their children, nor children put to death for their parents;

each will die for their own sin" (Deuteronomy 24:16). The school is responsible for the children through the contract that is signed and because it takes on legal responsibilities. For example, Garcia v. City of New York (1996) held that schools, once they take over physical custody and control of children, effectively take the place of their parents and guardians to both control and protect them. But schools have responsibilities beyond the parent because they act as representatives of the state. In this relationship, the Head takes a leadership role for her or his faculty and staff and has responsibility for mission delivery.

We would thus say that the parents' task is to choose a school that is consistent with their ambition for their child(ren). This is usually epitomized by the school's mission and values and felt through the sense of community the Christian school has. Once that choice is made, the parent does not relinquish responsibility to support the school to effectively educate the child. At the same time, the parent must now submit to the school's authority, given to it both by the parent and the state: "Have confidence in your leaders and submit to their authority, because they keep watch over you as those who must give an account. Do this so that their work will be a joy, not a burden, for that would be of no benefit to you" (Hebrews 13:17).

That authority is localized in the Head, who has been appointed by the Board of Trustees and who has the power to both accept and reject a student. This authority is not unlimited however, because at the end of each day the school gives the child back to the parent. This is why it is the Cord Principle – the 3 cords cannot be untangled without causing great harm to the child. The 3 cords must cooperate on the basis of mission and the Child Principle. When such cooperation exists, we typically experience the most powerful outcomes in the child's life.

Appendix 2: What Is the Job of the Board President?

Your leadership is a key part of your school's success. This is so in 2 ways:

1. You must lead the Board itself. The word "leader" in the New Testament is not a happy one – it refers almost always to those who were trying to kill Jesus and his followers! But the job of a leader is clear: "I appeal to you, brothers and sisters, in the name of our Lord Jesus Christ, that all of you agree with one another in what you say and that there be no divisions among you, but that you be perfectly united in mind and thought. My brothers and sisters, some from Chloe's household have informed me that there are quarrels among you. What I mean is this: One of you says, 'I follow Paul'; another, 'I follow Apollos'; another, 'I follow Cephas'; still another, 'I follow Christ'" (1 Corinthians 1: 10-12). In the context of the school this means you must:
   - Ensure a constancy of vision through knowing, understanding, and fulfilling the mission.
   - Make the mission concrete by creating a Strategic Plan that embodies both the mission of

the school and the Head of School's vision for where the school is going on its journey.
- Ensure that your fellow Trustees exercise discipline and patience in carrying out that plan.
- Teach your fellow Trustees that this plan has in mind the generations of students yet to come, not the current families.
- Model good attendance; participate with honesty and respect in the Board discussions; work hard on a committee; celebrate God's goodness in the school; pray daily for the students, faculty, and staff; give to the school.
- Teach the Board its responsibilities:
  - being strategic, not operational;
  - having and using a current Strategic Plan;
  - ensuring the development of Strategic Financial Management that details how the Strategic Plan can be afforded over time;
  - moving the school in a fiscally sound direction;
  - raising money;
  - developing the facilities to meet the needs of a changing education;
  - maintaining the facilities in an excellent state of repair; and
  - supporting and evaluating the Head of School, its only employee.
2. You must be the Head of School's partner in the work. I'm always struck that Jesus never sent people out on their own. "After this the Lord appointed seventy-two others and sent them two by two ahead of him to every town and place where he was about to go" (Luke 10:1). So it is with you and the school's operations leader. The Head does not have a peer within the school – they are all her employees. You

Appendix 2: What Is the Job of the Board President?

must be a peer that she can trust, can depend on, can gain guidance from, and can know that you hold her in your prayers at all times. Specifically:
- Meet with the school leader at least once every 2 weeks for lunch or a similar get-together to talk about business, but even more to create a relationship that deepens and in which business can be carried out in a far more effective way.
- Support the school leader in public at all times.
- Maintain absolute confidentiality so that conversations can be open, honest, and frank.
- Make evaluation of the school leader a function more of support than of measurement, i.e., establish achievable goals largely through the use of the Board's Strategic Plan, identify how success is measured, ensure the school leader has the resources to be successful.
- Ensure the Board does not interfere in the Head of School's operational autonomy on a day to day basis – clearly identify the areas that constitute that operational autonomy:
  - curriculum,
  - schedule,
  - calendar,
  - hiring and firing,
  - faculty performance,
  - the operations budget,
  - financial aid,
  - enrollment, and
  - marketing.
- Train your successor so that succession is carried out as seamlessly as possible.

Being a Board President is a great privilege. It is also a position of considerable power. You should exercise that power as a servant leader, continuing to grow in knowledge and wisdom about schools and your school in particular. You are a steward of what God has given you. "Each of you should use whatever gift you have received to serve others, as faithful stewards of God's grace in its various forms. If anyone speaks, they should do so as one who speaks the very words of God. If anyone serves, they should do so with the strength God provides, so that in all things God may be praised through Jesus Christ. To him be the glory and the power for ever and ever. Amen" (1 Peter 4: 10-11). Be a joyful leader knowing that following Jesus means that he is with you and with your school to be a blessing to your children.

Appendix 3: The Servant Leader Principle: Christian Management / Leadership

"Jesus knew that the Father had put all things under his power, and that he had come from God and was returning to God; so he got up from the meal, took off his outer clothing, and wrapped a towel around his waist. . . . When he had finished washing their feet, he put on his clothes and returned to his place. 'Do you understand what I have done for you?' he asked them" (John 13: 3-4, 12).

Christian school leaders are servant leaders. They have the following obligations:

- Serve the mission of the school – everything else is a subset of this.
- Serve the children of the school as the primary client.
- Recruit and support faculty and staff to:
  - provide resources;
  - be present for them and know each one;
  - be in an ongoing conversation with them;
  - help them grow throughout their careers;

- hold them accountable; and
- let them go when they are unable to fulfill their task with excellence.
- Partner with the Board for effective planning.
- Execute the plan with diligence and efficiency.

Authority and service seem to always be in tension. If I am in authority, how can I at the same time be in service? As the Head of School or Division Leader or Business Manager, where is authority and where is service? How do they link?

Authority is not to be denied. It is there for 3 important purposes: to know and do a job in such a way that people follow; to hold others accountable; to bring a key perspective to conversations and thus enrich decision making. Each of these purposes is part of leadership.

To be obvious, you can't be a leader unless you have followers. Gaining followers happens in a variety of ways, as history shows: the "strong" individual, the mystic, the rich person, the visionary, the person of power, and so on. Most of these are not servant leaders. It is important to know that – servant leadership is only one of many ways to lead. We consider it to be the highest form of leadership.

In a school, servant leadership operates at every level. The teacher needs to lead children from being subordinates to becoming followers as quickly as possible and does that through building relationships, demonstrating competence, teaching with passion, and having an expansive vision of where each child can go. The administrator optimally serves followers who are similarly committed to the mission of the school, are supported in their growing competence, trust in the leader, are held accountable, and contribute to the whole as members of a productive team. The Head serves the team by optimizing and expanding its strengths. Gallup, the polling organization, found that the 4 needs of followers were trust, compassion, stability, hope. In the Christian school, these words have resonance as well. Still, we might rewrite them in this form:

Gallup	Christian School
Trust	Competence and making and keeping promises
Compassion	Love – desiring always the best for the other
Stability	Knowing that Jesus is the Rock and standing securely there
Hope	Mission, planning, execution

Leadership does not always operate according to the organization chart. Formal leadership is often supported by informal leadership in the organization – the exemplary teacher who leads conversations, presents at conferences, and chairs committees has an authority far beyond her title. Informal leadership is the place where we discover those who have the servant's heart. While we may hire those who already have titles and / or reputations, we see in the everyday interactions of each person much more clearly what his or her impulse to action is – whether to power or to service.

Robert Greenleaf of the Greenleaf Center for Servant Leadership wrote: "The servant-leader is servant first . . . It begins with the natural feeling that one wants to serve, to serve first. Then conscious choice brings one to aspire to lead. That person is sharply different from one who is leader first, perhaps because of the need to assuage an unusual power drive or to acquire material possessions . . . The leader-first and the servant-first are 2 extreme types. Between them there are shadings and blends that are part of the infinite variety of human nature. The difference manifests itself in the care taken by the servant-first to make sure that other people's highest priority needs are being served. The best test, and difficult to administer, is: Do those served grow as persons? Do they, while being served, become healthier, wiser, freer, more autonomous, more likely themselves to become servants? And, what is the effect on the least privileged in society? Will they benefit or at least not be further deprived?"

This leads to the key observation that for the Christian school, servant leadership has an objective that is clear and non-negotiable. At the heart of the word "service" is the person of the child. We are not in our schools to serve everyone equally. Far from it. First is the child, who is the reason for the school, its mission outcome, and the most vulnerable person in the school community. Servant leadership is thus not even-handed. Within the context of the school, each servant leader serves first the student. Both the adult leader and the adult follower must know that their contract obligation to fulfill their responsibilities in return for various benefits is the legal mirror for their moral obligation to deliver the mission to the student.

The practical issues that arise are difficult in practice, while clear in theory. What happens if adults do not do their jobs well? How do we hold adults accountable for that mission delivery, irrespective of whether that is in the Business Office, in the classroom, on the playing fields, on field trips or in the Advancement Office? What about that beloved member of the church community who happens to be a mediocre teacher or administrator? Does servant leadership imply that we place adult community as the prime concern? Is rocking the boat being a servant? Should we overlook adult misconduct because we genuinely do care for every member of the school?

This would suggest that "servant" is a soft term with no substance. To the contrary – when we recognize that the center of our attention is the child, to serve the child implies that we are all accountable in the most demanding ways both personally and collectively. In that collective sense, it is the school that takes on the responsibility for mission delivery to each child. Thus, the school must corporately take on the characteristic of servant leader to fully develop each child's God-given gifts and fulfill God's purpose in each child's life. Adults thus operate in 2 ways. The first is as an individual where the servant leader seeks to deliver the mission to the child and support, enhance, and develop the skills of each employee. The second is as a school body exhibiting corporately the servant leader disposition. Here, the requirement that each individual be a contributing element to that corporate identity is key.

If we are committed as servant leaders merely to the individual employee, it would be possible to imagine the needs of the adult becoming, as often happens in our schools, equivalent to or even greater than the needs of the child. Where, however, we are committed as servant leader institutionally to the child, now each adult has a critical role to play and for which to be held accountable. Being a servant leader is thus not just an individual but a corporate responsibility. Note that 1 Corinthians 12 is implacable that we all play a part in the body of Christ and, implicitly, in whatever station of life we have been led to. "Even so the body is not made up of one part but of many" (verse 14).

The Head as servant leader primarily for the child must therefore root out adult incompetence and ensure that the child receives the best mission-centered education. Similarly, the Board of Trustees must hold the Head accountable. Once the highest needs of the child have been taken care of, and in order to achieve that goal, the adult is also nurtured and fed. Accountability is thus a key element of being a servant leader.

"Jesus called them together and said, 'You know that the rulers of the Gentiles lord it over them, and their high officials exercise authority over them. Not so with you. Instead, whoever wants to become great among you must be your servant, and whoever wants to be first must be your slave—just as the Son of Man did not come to be served, but to serve, and to give his life as a ransom for many'" (Matthew 20:25-28).

The Christian school is an exemplar of servant leadership. We give our lives as a school body to deliver the mission to the student. We are held accountable for the excellence of that delivery. I individually deliver the mission and am held individually accountable. When the Christian school functions in this healthy way, it can achieve excellence.

Appendix 4: What Is Your Job as Head of School?

The Head of School's job has 3 elements, and we will discuss each in turn:

1. Provide the Vision
2. Grow the Community
3. Lead the Board with the Board President

Provide the Vision

The Board's job is to think strategically on behalf of the next generation. This idea of generation is deeply Biblical. Right from the beginning of Scripture, we come into contact with God's desire for all generations – He knows it's a process and a long one at that. "And God said, 'This is the sign of the covenant I am making between me and you and every living creature with you, a covenant for all generations to come: I have set my rainbow in the clouds, and it will be the sign of the covenant between me and the earth'" (Genesis 9:12-13).

Trustees and the Head of School must operate in the present but in the context of future generations. They express that thinking through the Strategic Plan that imagines where the school will be some years into the future

– when several of the Board members will no longer even be on the Board. But how can they think strategically as part-time volunteers who are not experts in education?

It is the Head of School who must provide the vision upon which the Strategic Plan is developed. Many Heads come into a school with a vision already pre-planned. We encourage you to take a pause and wait until you've been with the school at least 2 years. First, get to know the children, learn who the community is, understand the strengths and challenges of the people who are working at the school, appreciate the parents, interrogate the finances, look at the structures. Even if you are hired from within, the view from the Head's office is different from the view as an academic or business administrator. Be patient. Unless the school is in crisis, take time to reflect, think, consult. During that time of reflection and understanding, the vision comes:

- Through times of quiet and reflection and prayer apart from the group. Jesus often sought solitude to pray and be with his Father in a way that was not possible in the middle of the crowds, e.g., Luke 5:33 and 6:12.
- Through conversation with the Board President, mature school leaders, and mentor(s). When there were matters of great importance in the early church to discover the vision for moving forward, they always met in council to talk with each other, advise and admonish, and come to agreement for moving forward. The first of these was in Jerusalem, Acts 15 ff.
- Through experience. Our previous experience is a double-edged sword. It can certainly be influential in a good way by showing what worked and did not work. It can also teach the wrong lessons or lessons that are misapplied in this new situation.

Nonetheless, we rightly use experience (including our professional training and ongoing professional reading and instruction) to inform our vision. This is particularly so for us as Christians since we constantly look backward in order to understand how to move forward. Jesus did that very thing when on the road to Emmaus in Luke 24: 27.

- Through intuition. Intuition is something we employ, often even when we deny we're employing it! Having "a hunch" about the right way to go is often the brain's way of organizing information in patterns that give us great insight. It also can be problematic and lead us down the wrong path. Nonetheless, we do well to listen to the voice within and take it into account in our vision casting.
- Through "trying out" or testing our vision with people we trust – those who tend to agree with us as well as those who tend to be excellent critics. In these conversations or exchanges of emails, we can find what the challenges might be and ensure that we have thought about them, even if there no obvious solutions right now. "Do not quench the Spirit. Do not treat prophecies with contempt but test them all; hold on to what is good, reject every kind of evil" (1 Thessalonians 5).

Visioning is key for you as Head of School. While it might be really straightforward and obvious – e.g., we need to increase enrollment – it may equally be multi-faceted and not obvious at all. With our vision clearly in our mind, tested in prayer and reflection, conversation, intuition, experience, and testing, you can go to the Board with confidence and ask to have the vision put into a strategic planning form.

Grow the Community

CSM thinks of leadership from a servant leadership perspective. As Jesus puts it: "The Son of Man did not come to be served, but to serve" (Matthew 20). In educational terms, it means that the Head is there to support the faculty and staff. The Head:

- provides resources;
- is present for them and knows each one;
- is in an ongoing conversation with them; and
- helps them grow throughout their careers.

Teaching is an arduous profession that more resembles a marathon than a sprint. The teacher, having become comfortable with the process of teaching over the first 5 years, then looks forward to 30 to 40 years of the "same." It is a flat profession. There is no career ladder, no advancement except to go into administration. The pay structure is usually not inspired either – a ladder that stops at 20 years and then looks forward to 20 years of cost-of-living increases. And all this exists in an environment of vocally demanding parents, children who are more challenging than they were 20 years ago, and a social / economic environment that gives the teacher no certainty in answering the question: What am I preparing my students for?

The school leader who thinks that leadership means more and more new initiatives is destined to failure and resistance, even hostility from the teachers and staff. This is one reason why the longevity of our Heads of School is so short!

Instead, the servant leader within the constraints of mission, vision, and strategic planning, listens, encourages, provides resources, acts as the cheerleader, eliminates obstacles, inspires excellence. The intent of this servant leader work is to support the teacher in constant growing. If the teacher does not grow, the teacher cannot serve the child. If the teacher does not grow, the experience of teaching becomes more arduous and ultimately results in cynicism. If the teacher does not grow, then her students will not be excellent. If the teacher does not grow, her colleagues cannot be excellent.

So, the servant leader serves each faculty member within the context of the whole faculty culture. Growth of 1 = growth and excellence of all = student excellence = motivation = longevity. St. Peter says in 1 Peter 2: "Therefore, rid yourselves of all malice and all deceit, hypocrisy, envy, and slander of every kind. Like newborn babies, crave pure spiritual milk, so that by it you may grow up in your salvation, now that you have tasted that the Lord is good." If we were to rewrite that for teachers, we might say: "Therefore, rid yourselves of obstinacy, adult-centeredness, hanging onto the past, gossip, self-satisfaction. As if you were just coming out of teacher's college again, crave excellence in your pedagogy and spiritual maturity in your relationships with students and with colleagues. Aspire to continually grow so that you can serve better and better, for Jesus the Teacher / Rabbi goes ahead."

This is not to ignore the authority of the servant leader (Mark 1:27). The servant leader has authority precisely because she is a servant first. In Matthew 20, there is the story of the mother of the sons of Zebedee who wanted her sons to be first in the kingdom of heaven. Jesus calls all the disciples and patiently outlines it again as he has before and will again after: "You know that the rulers of the Gentiles lord it over them, and their high officials exercise authority over them. Not so with you. Instead, whoever wants to become great among you must be your servant, and whoever wants to be first must be your slave – just as the Son of Man did not come to be served, but to serve, and to give his life as a ransom for many." It is the suffering servant who has the authority to forgive sins and heal – and change the rules about the Sabbath. It is being a servant leader that gives you the authority to hold the faculty member (and staff member) to high standards. They, too, must exhibit the attitude of the servant leader in their various settings. The faculty member has a particular challenge in teaching (cf. James 3) and is held to particularly high standards since the future of the child may well be influenced forever by the teacher's actions and words. The Head of School must:

- hold them accountable and
- let them go when they are unable to fulfill their task with excellence.

Letting people go – firing them – is no one's favorite task, and we don't wish to gloss over the difficulties of doing it. It is nonetheless part of the servant leader's responsibility to recognize that the Head of School serves first the child and only then the adult. Where the child is in jeopardy academically and / or relationally, then the teacher must go. It is a scandal that we do not have the courage to understand the sometimes-long-lasting damage done to a child by a teacher who cannot lead effectively in the classroom, on the field or stage, or on the wider canvas of the child's life. Typically, these events will happen because the person refuses to grow in a meaningful way.

The authority of the Head / servant leader is predicated on supporting the teacher in professional growth and increasing insight. St. Paul says in 1 Thessalonians 3:12: "May the Lord make your love increase and overflow for each other and for everyone else, just as ours does for you." In the school, "love" equates to ensuring that the teacher can serve the child with increasing and overflowing skill and insight.

The authority of the Head is seen in the Head's willingness to continually know and find out whether the faculty (and staff) are doing a job with excellence, hold them accountable to it, and release them from the school when they are no longer an asset for the children. As it says in Romans 13:4: "For the one in authority is God's servant for your good. But if you do wrong, be afraid, for rulers do not bear the sword for no reason." We should not fear our own authority if we have first been the servant.

Lead the Board with the Board President

Through vision and servant leadership promoting the growth of the community, the Head of School provides the Board with both the basis for strategic planning and the confidence that the Board's work will be supported successfully at the school operations level. The Head's most important strategic relationship is with the Board President. We know that in our Christian schools, the effectiveness of the school is often compromised, jeopardized, and occasionally reversed by the impact of a Board that doesn't understand its job. The job of the Board President (see Entheos Vol. 1 No. 1) is to lead the Board and be the School Head's partner. How can the School Head help the Board President in leading the Board?

The CSM Cord Principle states that the Head is "the guardian of the child's healthy development, the proactive partner with the parent, and the sustainer of the teacher's Godly genius." Further, the Cord Principle speaks to the importance of the Board. "The Board establishes the mission, hires the Head of School, plans for the future and provides the resources (money and facilities) needed for that plan to succeed." This shows clearly that the roles are distinct, though not separate, and that effective leadership of the Board means ensuring each can carry out his or her own role – the Board in the strategic sphere and the Head in the operations sphere. The crossover of strategic and operations is led by the Head / Board President partnership. Their task is to align the Board's task with the Head's task through the Strategic Plan, providing clarity of direction for the Board's actions and clarity of action for the Head's priorities. This requires constant vigilance.

We also have to recognize that entities are translated by human beings. We encourage Heads and Board Presidents to be proactive in establishing and maintaining strong personal / professional relationships in order to build up the school and sustain it over time (cf. 1 Corinthians 14:26).

1. Meet together regularly – pray, break bread, reflect and work together.
2. Ensure there are no surprises in either direction through frank and open communication.
3. Build trust through developing commitments, fulfilling those commitments, and doing so professionally and wisely.

These 3 tasks of vision, growth, and leadership comprise the foundation for great Head of School leadership.

Appendix 5: The Ox Principle: Christian School Finances

1 Timothy 6: 17
"Do not muzzle an ox while it is treading out the grain"

Numbers 18: 21 (NIV)
"I give to the Levites all the tithes in Israel as their inheritance in return for the work they do while serving at the tent of meeting."

1 Timothy 6: 8
"Anyone who does not provide for their relatives, and especially for their own household, has denied the faith and is worse than an unbeliever."

Proverbs 22: 7
The rich rule over the poor, and the borrower is slave to the lender.

Exodus 41: 33-36
And now let Pharaoh look for a discerning and wise man and put him in charge of the land of Egypt. [34] Let Pharaoh appoint commissioners over the land

to take a fifth of the harvest of Egypt during the seven years of abundance. ³⁵ They should collect all the food of these good years that are coming and store up the grain under the authority of Pharaoh, to be kept in the cities for food. ³⁶ This food should be held in reserve for the country, to be used during the seven years of famine that will come upon Egypt, so that the country may not be ruined by the famine.

The Christian School thinks about money a lot. It enjoys the thought that God provides richly for his people. It wants to have the best resources it can to serve its children. It is neither embarrassed nor ashamed to talk about God's gift of money. It has an obligation to:

- Provide resources that allow it to deliver the mission with excellence.
- Balance its budget.
- Compensate its employees honorably and respectfully.
- Provide a safe and optimal learning environment.
- Minimize / eliminate debt.
- Maintain a reserve.

Let's start with the last bullet point first: maintain a reserve. The Minnesota Council of Non-Profits discovered that "nonprofits with minimal or no reserves were more likely to have cut budgets, eliminated staff positions, reduced wages and benefits. They were also less likely to have been able to increase services to respond to growing demand." That is, if your school has no cash reserves, it is in a constantly bad place whether it is to respond to economic hard times in a healthy way or to respond to economic good times by being able to take advantage of opportunities. And there is no justification in the Christian school for taking the attitude that the Lord will provide. Certainly there are times when the widow's jar of oil stays miraculously full. And we rejoice in the goodness of our God. At the same time, it is clear that trust can often (often!) be a misnomer for poor management with the result that our schools go out of business because they lacked the cardinal virtue of prudence. Aristotle defined prudence as *recta ratio agibilium*, "right reason applied to practice." And St. Thomas Aquinas considered it the first of the virtues. When we apply prudence with the guidance of the Holy Spirit, it may well lead us to take steps that may appear foolish from a worldly point of view – but that does not include the lack of foresight. Our God is a God of planning. Jeremiah 29:10 says, "For I know the plans I have for you," declares the Lord, "plans to prosper you and not to harm you, plans to give you hope and a future." Indeed, it is the ungodly who fail to plan: "let us eat and drink . . . for tomorrow we die" (Isaiah 22:13). Interestingly, that planning often meant that the great Christian leaders have often had to operate by faith that the plan would come to pass and not in their own life-times. So it is with our schools. Reserves are one of the ways in which the Christian school exercises prudence and foresight in order to ensure that the school will still be here for the next generation. Whether used or not in "my" time of service, they will provide Joseph's sustenance in the time of famine.

With that in mind, we can turn to the issue of the school's budget. Talking about money for the Christian school always begins with the school's mission. Many commentators have said that we should begin with the end in mind, and it is good advice. We would take it one step further and say that the end of the Christian school – its mission – is what dictates its budget. Let there be no error here. Budget for many Christian schools means eking out a painful existence on the backs of poorly paid workers and badly maintained buildings. We don't have to go to the prosperity preachers to know that this is bad economics of body, mind, and spirit. There is no Christian character in being paid below the poverty level or not having the resources to teach with the right materials or passing the buck down the road by not doing the upkeep of buildings and grounds that should be done today. The question thus becomes whether we believe in delivering the mission at a level of excellence and what that means. CSM believes that we are called to excellence, and that we witness that to our own people/community as well as to those who are watching us from the outside "But you are a chosen race, a royal priesthood, a holy nation, a people for his own possession, that you may proclaim the excellencies of him who called you out of darkness into his marvelous light" (1 Peter 2:9). Witnessing to excellence means exemplifying excellence in our own financial practices.

There are then very clear steps to take in thinking about the budget:

1. Understand your own mission statement – what does it mean when we apply the standard of 'excellence' to each of its words and think about the investment that is necessary to make that happen?
2. Don't assume that the budget you have had for so many years is, de facto, the best budget. In fact, assume that there are deficits that you want to improve over time. As school leaders, be aware that our followers (employees) will want to act sacrificially in order to support the mission of the school and to help as many students as possible. Applaud that and appreciate it. Don't let it stop the conversation that must also happen in order to support them appropriately in their mission delivery.
3. Unless the school is new, debt is typically the wrong way to raise money.

Appendix 5: The Ox Principle: Christian School Finances

    a. This includes lines of credit required because there is not enough money to get through the year – budgets must be balanced, and balanced by ensuring that the families who want this education pay for the expenses of the education through their tuition.
4. It also includes borrowing for It is just wrong not to compensate the Christian worker professionally. The notion that they should be "underpaid" because it is a ministry fails to honor them. Certainly it is a ministry. We will not try to define a fair wage. But we do know this: when our workers are paid in a way that does not allow them to raise a family, or that forces the "Christian" worker to be paid for by the spouse who works in a "secular" occupation, or that results in them not having benefits or any kind of retirement opportunities, then our budget lacks a moral foundation. We can go further and say that in order to attract and retain the best teachers and staff, we will pay them competitively, recognizing their value and honoring it.
    b. building improvements and new construction where the money should be raised through fund-raising.
    c. Debt payments are a tax on tuition and degrades the school's budget.

A note about fund-raising: CSM believes that the school's operational expenses must be paid for through tuition and fees. Fund-raising is the gift of the heart that invests in the future of the school and to the direct benefit of the children. God has made us generous people. It is part of the way in which we are created. The school should joyfully ask its supporters for their gifts given because of God's generosity to us.

We are committed to being great stewards of the riches that God gives to us. We need to think of God as generous and thus that He will meet our needs. We have a responsibility to express those needs in such a way that we exemplify excellence in our mission delivery, professionally pay and provide benefits to our people, maintain prudence in our reserves and debt management, and balance the budget. That is the Ox Principle.

Appendix 6: The Mary Principle: Philanthropy in the Christian School

Luke 8: 3
"Mary (called Magdalene) from whom seven demons had come out; Joanna the wife of Chuza, the manager of Herod's household; Susanna; and many others. These women were helping to support them out of their own means."

Christian Schools need supporters who will give of their abundance (at whatever level that indicates) in order to further the work of the school. While parents can be expected to pay tuition and fees for the services they receive, that money typically does not purchase property, build facilities, or provide items that are over and above normal everyday expenses. It is thus very important that Christian schools:

- Raise money over and above operating income.
- Exercise and teach philanthropy.
- Develop a culture of philanthropy.

- Treat donors honorably and respectfully.
- Follow the highest ethical standards.

It is no casual statement to call this the Mary Principle. The women mentioned in Luke's Gospel had been "cured of evil spirits and diseases" (verse 2). They had experienced an astonishing change in their circumstances and were giving, we might assume, out of gratitude for deliverance. We can assume that these women were also the same ones who, in Luke 23 and 24, gave Jesus' body its final ministrations and were the first at the tomb the next day. Certainly, having someone as wealthy as Joanna in the ranks would have been enormously important in order to cover the expenses of this work. Mary Magdalene is so important that she is mentioned at least 12 times, more than many of the apostles, and mentioned in connection with the key events of Jesus' life. These women were not just appurtenances, but key and vital members of Jesus' work with characteristics that one might find in other passages such as Proverbs 31. Connecting philanthropy to these women is to establish important points about the work of raising money for Christian schools. There are five operating principles that the Lukan narrative identifies:

1. Giving is in gratitude for what has been done.
2. Giving is done by people who are intimately involved with the action.
3. Giving includes involvement, not just the act of giving itself.
4. Giving galvanizes possibilities that otherwise could not be imagined.
5. Giving is recognized and honored.

We don't know if these women were asked to give or if they initiated the conversation. We can imagine, however,

Appendix 6: The Mary Principle: Philanthropy in the Christian School

that once someone like Joanna had been healed, she asked in what way she could be part of what was going on with Jesus. There was obviously some kind of organizational structure to Jesus' ministry such that when he arrived at a place, there had been some preparations: food bought for the road, fresh clothing to replace what was wearing out, new sandals on occasion, even transportation such as the special time that Jesus told his disciples to seek out the ass for his entrance into Jerusalem. It can't have been a simple thing for 13 men and other followers to travel around the countryside living a peripatetic lifestyle. Joanna would have been gratefully welcomed into the company of donors who kept things on an even keel. Maybe she asked; maybe she was asked. What we do know is that she and others (many others) were thought important enough to be specifically honored through Luke's narrative.

Giving for Christian education needs to follow these five principles. Unfortunately, caring for the money of others has not been a strong practice on the part of Christian schools. Christian donors often (very often) become disillusioned because their money, given thoughtfully and hopefully, vanishes into a black hole that has these characteristics:

- It is not well accounted for or accountable – how was it spent and what was it used for.
- It does not solve problems; in fact, it merely papers over the problems the school has and the school fails to address the issues it has. The consequence is that the need for the donation does not go away but reappears over and over again. The gift is seen in the present tense only.
- It does not move the school forward. It does not create space for creative solutions or visionary possibilities. In fact, the school refuses to acknowledge that the need for the gift suggests that the school

has any problems at all. Far from opening up opportunities, it reaffirms the school in thinking that their "faithful prayer" has been answered. The future is not a new day of creativity but only the present day repeated.
- It does not build capacity. The gift is used to plug the budget that currently exists. It does not fund those things that could help the administration, faculty, and staff of the school see any change in their own circumstances that would allow them to move the school forward: it does not fund significant professional development, the use of consulting services, professionalization of operations, technology systems to collect and manage data.

Thus, Christian schools must manage and think about gifts in a different way. Even the manna in the desert enabled the Jewish people to move towards the Promised Land! Christian schools must know how to look after the gift legally and ethically. Christian schools must know how to use the gift in a way that moves the school from the present into the future. Gifts that only serve the present, by definition, mask underlying management and leadership problems that the Board of Trustees and School Head are not addressing effectively. Gifts are about the future and about vision and about direction.

Interestingly, Christian schools are also bad about asking people for money. It would seem that Jesus and his disciples were not shy about it. Mary, Joanna, and many others supported their work. The Mary Principle suggests that many want to support the work of Jesus in the Christian school. Penelope Burk in her research into giving says that, for example, "9 to 10 percent of people say they have put bequests in their wills, but more than 30 percent say they would definitely do it or take under serious consideration

Appendix 6: The Mary Principle: Philanthropy in the Christian School

if asked." It is clear that our schools do not have the confidence, or they do not think it is right, to ask their potential supporters for money. There is sometimes the thought that these people SHOULD give and we shouldn't have to ask them. We do not take a position on that. What we do know is that if the school does not ask them, many who would will not. After all, they ARE being asked by many other organizations and individuals, sometimes on a weekly basis, to contribute to many worthy causes.

The Christian school needs philanthropic dollars. It is not a "love of money" that leads to asking for money. It is an appreciation of the need to serve the children of the school and carry out its mission. It is because the school can clearly and authentically identify a future-oriented need. It is done with complete integrity and open accountability. It is done transparently and without embarrassment. It is done with the operating budget taken care of – it is not a replacement for good daily management and accounting practices.

From the donor's perspective, the gift is given because it has been asked for. The donor feels that their philanthropy is an excellent investment in the future. Donors equally feel that they are honored in their giving – firstly, by being asked within the context of a plan; secondly, by being included appropriately in the conversation; thirdly, by being thanked, told that their gift was used as asked, and given evidence that children benefited. Finally, the donor is treated in a way that makes them want to be equally or more generous the following year. A 'tired' donor is typically someone for whom these things have not happened.

The Mary Principle is built on the Ox Principle. The school that balances its budget, limits its debt, compensates its employees professionally, and has a reserve is a school that will raise the most money. The school that manages its budget poorly, fails to charge tuition that pays the bills, goes into debt, and asks its employees to work "sacrificially" i.e., without the ability to raise their families, will raise the least money. These two principles work hand in hand.

Every Christian family that is involved with a Christian school wants to support it. The Mary Principle, and the Ox Principle that underlies it, gives them every opportunity to do so. They will be eager and excited to see the miracles of what God has given them translate into the miracles that God will perform through their school.

Appendix 7: The Child Principle: the Christian School

Matthew 19:14
Jesus said, "Let the little children come to me, and do not hinder them, for the kingdom of heaven belongs to such as these."

Mark 10:14
When Jesus saw this, he was indignant. He said to them, "Let the little children come to me, and do not hinder them, for the kingdom of God belongs to such as these.

Luke 18:16
But Jesus called the children to him and said, "Let the little children come to me, and do not hinder them, for the kingdom of God belongs to such as these.

Matthew 18:3-5
And he said: "Truly I tell you, unless you change and become like little children, you will never enter the kingdom of heaven. Therefore, whoever takes the lowly position of this child is the greatest in the

kingdom of heaven. And whoever welcomes one such child in my name welcomes me.

As the Christian school strives to implement the Child Principle, it recognizes that all three of the Synoptic gospels tell adults to stop getting in the child's way. The Child Principle requires the Christian school to:

- Put the child first (be student-centered).
- Instruct adults to meet the child where the child is first, before requiring the child to meet the adult where the adult is.
- Recognize that authority is there to serve the child, not to lord it over the child.

We need to be clear that child-centeredness is operating with the child at the center under the authority of God. Being child-centered should never be considered outside of the context of God's love and grace. First comes the recognition that we believe in God and that knowledge of God is primary: "Only be careful, and watch yourselves closely so that you do not forget the things your eyes have seen or let them fade from your heart as long as you live. Teach them to your children and to their children after them." (Deuteronomy 4:9). The cry to not forget is key to our status as a religion that is embedded in a teleological history centered in incarnation and resurrection.

But when we think of the child within the context of the Christian school, it does not take a long look to recognize that adults create school often to their own benefit, not to the primary benefit of the child. Let's think of a couple of actual examples:

- We create schedules that fit the convenience of teachers and administrators rather than the clear needs of the child.
- We teach in a way that is comfortable for me and reflecting my one style rather than fitting and meeting the needs of each child and their many styles.
- We allocate time to meet bureaucratic requirements and arbitrary rules (such as the 120-hour Carnegie Unit) rather than considering how much time – more or less – makes sense from the child's point of view.

We must remember that school is a mandatory place for children but an optional place for adults; it is a place where children have little or no power and adults have much. Children continually move through and have no necessary sense of permanence while adults might stay for an entire career / vocation. It can be a place where well-meaning disciples "hinder" the children from coming to the Father.

Being child-centered makes us sensitive to our adult self-centeredness. Indeed, it is only within the context of God's love and grace that leaving the self-centeredness of adults behind makes any sense and, indeed, is possible. When we are able to stop being self-centered as adults, we are freed to become immersed in the lives of our children. Then, we can "teach (the laws) to your children, talking about them when you sit at home and when you walk along the road, when you lie down and when you get up" (Deut. 11.19). This all-encompassing embrace of the teaching life is what turns it from mere career into vocation.

Of course, God takes the same approach, considering us His children, embracing us and being with us (Emmanuel) through the indwelling of the Holy Spirit, through the law written on our hearts, through the reality of knowing we are created beings, and teaching us (Ps. 25: 4-5; 27:11; 32:8; 86:11; 94:10; 119). He was with us at the beginning of time teaching the man (Gen. 2: 16) while in Eden and apprenticing the man and woman in the making of clothing (Gen. 3:21). He came to us in Jesus, a child teaching in the Temple (Luke 2:46) and a man teaching the multitudes. In our schools we must note that God came to Adam and Eve within His creation and Jesus comes to us within the context of our lives. This is our model of how we should approach children – within the context of their own lives teaching them where they are and in the way that they can understand.

Child-centeredness thus asks us to leave behind our own adult selfishness (which scripturally is always attached to ambition, cf. 2 Cor. 12:20; Gal. 5:20; Phil. 2:3; James 3:14). It asks us to come towards the child within the child's own context and in a way that makes sense to the child. And it asks us to exercise authority in order to serve the child, not to dominate the child. We are reminded in our speaking of authority that Jesus remarked that we should receive the kingdom of God "like a child" (Mark 10:15) or not enter in. His last evening with his disciples was spent teaching them about foot washing. ""Do you understand what I have done for you?" he asked them. [13] "You call me 'Teacher' and 'Lord,' and rightly so, for that is what I am. [14] Now that I, your Lord and Teacher, have washed your feet, you also should wash one another's feet" (John 13: 12-14). Our authority is then to serve, a paradox in any age but no less in our own where authority means to lord it over others and exercise privilege.

None of this is to take away the difference between an adult and a child, the person who has been trained and the one who has not, the administrator who has been promoted from the one who has not. All these reflect our talents and gifts (given to us) and their developmental and temperamental growth (which is what we do with them at various ages). It is not to take away the authority that has the sense of judgment – there are plenty of places to go in Scripture to demonstrate the validity of that. But in our schools, the dominant impulse is always to look at education from the child's point of view, through the child's eyes, and with the child's best interests at heart. The dominant impulse is, thus, to love.

In our schools, that means actually paying deep attention to what we say we are doing and what we are actually doing; to recognizing our missions as being almost exclusively and correctly about helping the child; to asking children their thoughts, fears, dreams, aspirations and finding them of value and acting on them; to beginning each conversation with the admonition to keeping the child at the center; to coming to decisions and asking the question as to whom the decision primarily benefits; to running meetings that focus on mission delivery to the child, whatever the topic of conversation.

Schools with children at the center are fun, happy, high achieving, extraordinary places. Adults in them are vocation driven, selfless, wise, pure. James warns against being a teacher, noting how many pitfalls there are. But for those who know that is their calling, he also encourages in James 3: [13] "Who is wise and understanding among you? Let them show it by their good life, by deeds done in the humility that comes from wisdom. [14] But if you harbor bitter envy and selfish ambition in your hearts, do not boast about it or deny the truth. [17] But the wisdom that comes from heaven is first of all pure; then peace-loving, considerate, submissive, full of mercy and good fruit, impartial and sincere." That is the Child Principle.

Appendix 8: Books and Articles Cited

Burk, P. (2003) **Donor-Centered Fundraising: How to Hold on to Your Donors and Raise Much More Money** Ontario, Canada: Cygnus Applied Research

Collins, J. (2001) **Good to Great: Why Some Companies Make the Leap and Others Don't** New York: HarperBusiness

Corsello, J. and Minor, D. (2017) **Workspaces** Massachusetts: Harvard Business Review

Hill, A., Mellon, L., Laker, B., and Goddard, J. (2017) **The One Type of Leader Who Can Turn Around a Failing School** Massachusetts: Harvard Business Review

Johnson, S.K. (2008) **I second that emotion: Effects of emotional contagion and affect at work on leader and follower outcomes** Science Direct: The Leadership Quarterly 19 (2008) 1–19

NBOA, Measuring Success, ISM (2017) **Effects of Tuition Increases on Enrollment Demand: an updated study** last downloaded July 30, 2018 https://www.netassets.org/viewdocument/effects-of-tuition-increases-on-enr

Rivkin, S. G., Hanushek, E. A., and Kain, J. F. (2005) **Teachers, Schools, and Academic Achievement** Econometrica 73, 2

Rockoff, J. E. **The Impact of Individual Teachers on Students' Achievement: Evidence from Panel Data** (2004) American Economic Review 94, 2

Sanders, W. L., and Rivers, J. C. (1996) **Cumulative and Residual Effects of Teachers on Future Student Academic Achievement** Knoxville, TN: University of Tennessee Value-Added Research and Assessment Center

Scott, S. (2002) **Fierce Conversations** New York: Penguin Group

Stone, D., Patton, B., and Heen, S. (1999) **Difficult Conversations** New York: Penguin Books

God's Inspired Word through and in the Holy Bible